A Keepsake

JOURNAL

———•———

Grandpa, Do You Remember When?
Sharing a Lifetime of Loving Memories

Homer Eldridge

Fulton Books, Inc.
Meadville, PA

Published by Fulton Books 2019

Paintings by: Jim Daly

ISBN 978-1-64654-031-0 (paperback)
ISBN 978-1-64654-032-7 (digital)

Printed in the United States of America

In loving memory of Virginia "Mema" Norman
Eldridge (April 2, 1935–December 7, 2017)

Wife, mother, grandmother, and friend

ASLEEP

I've closed my eyes and fallen asleep;
There is no reason for you to weep.
This is a debt we all must pay.
But it is a sweet and peaceful way.
I've endured pain and sometimes sorrow;
Now I don't have to worry about tomorrow.
But life for you must go on.
You must not worry because I'm gone.
You stood beside me all the way.
When I was down, you knew what to say.
You always told me to get some rest.
Let me sleep now; I've done my best.
So please now let me rest in peace;
The tears you're shedding soon will cease.
You'll soon realize that this was meant to be;
And I thank God because He came for me.

DEDICATION

This book is dedicated to my longtime partner; confidant, best friend, and wife (since April 25, 1953)—Virginia Norman Eldridge (aka Mema)—and my four precious boys, without whom I would not have had the determination, interest, or ambition to write this for my boys: Christopher (Punkin) Eldridge, Bradley Warren, Cameron Eldridge, and last but not least, Blake Warren. These boys have been such an inspiration to Mema and me since they were given to us by our Lord. He can deliver some precious cargo from time to time, and He did it on each occasion of their birth. I thank and praise the Lord for that gift. I also want to thank the Lord for all He has done for me throughout the many years of my travels; He has been there every step of the way.

CONTENTS

SHORT STORIES OF OUR FAMILY THAT YOU MAY LIKE

MY MILITARY CAREER

PREFACE FOR MY FOUR BOYS TO THE BOOK *GRANDPA, DO YOU REMEMBER WHEN?*

Papa will attempt to answer all questions asked by you through the book given to me at Christmas a couple of years ago. I have answered the questions to the best of my ability and truthfully. The book did not provide adequate space for my answers, so I have written my answers in exact form as presented to me; and by the Grace of God, they are my true feelings. In all cases, the questions were asked to a grandpa; however, in many cases, I have answered for both Mema and me as she has been a great part of my life and I could not have had the success that I have without her being by my side helping me all the way. Mema has been my best and most inspiring inspiration throughout my life since we met in high school. I pray that all of you will realize that it is much better to work together as a team than struggle against one another. May the Lord continue to bless each of you in a powerful way and be the leader in your life as He was for us. I have certain memories of each of you individually, and each of you are a unique individual to us; and one is just as important to us as the other. Mema and Papa have always loved their boys, and hopefully, you have understood that from your early beginning. Hopefully, you will carry that thought and feeling on to the next level of your life and enjoy your family as much as we have ours.

GRANDPA: DO YOU REMEMBER WHEN?

OUR FAMILY TREE

GRANDPA, WHAT WERE THE NAMES OF YOUR GRANDMA AND GRANDPA?

Father's Side

Great-grandfather:	Reacie Layton Eldridge (paternal)	Born: Sep.25, 1853	Died: Dec. 30, 1929
Great-grandmother:	Ann Nipper (paternal)	Born:	Died:
Grandfather:	Homer Jackson Eldridge (paternal)	Born: Feb.19, 1885	Died: June 21, 1967
Grandmother:	Lelia Francis Eldridge (maternal)	Born: March 18, 1894	Died: 1917
Great-grandfather:	William Daniel Eldridge(maternal)	Born: Jan.31, 1852	Died: May 26, 1918

Mother's Side

Great-grandfather:	Miles Christopher Hodge	Born: Sep. 1845	Died:
Great-grandmother:	Lydia Jane Singletary	Born: May 22, 1865	Died: Nov. 7, 1936

HOMER ELDRIDGE

Grandfather:	Augustus F. Hodge	Born: March 27, 1893	Died: May 12, 1939
Grandmother:	Lizzie Thompson Hodge	Born:	Died: March 14, 1916
Step-Grandmother:	Eliza Geneva Cardin Hodge	Born: August 13, 1893	Died: May 29, 1973

GRANDPA, WHAT WERE THE NAMES OF YOUR PARENTS?

Father:	Everett Preston Eldridge	Born: July 6, 1915	Died: Aug. 13, 2000
Mother:	Anna Malinda Hodge Eldridge Ormston	Born: Sept.10, 1915	Died: Sept. 3, 1986
Stepmother:	Thelma Gertrude Hart	Born: Apr. 6, 1918	Died: Oct. 22, 1999
Stepfather:	Harold Ormston	Born: Nov. 9, 1903	Died: Oct. 15, 1992

HOW MANY BROTHERS AND SISTERS DID YOU HAVE?

Two (2) Brothers:	Everett Eugene (Gene) Eldridge	Born: June 15, 1936	Died:
	Reasie Augustus (Pat) Eldridge	Born: July 26, 1938	Died:
One (1) Sister:	Betty Ann Eldridge Sherertz Burke	Born: Dec. 11, 1931	Died:
One (1) Half Sister	Stillborn in 1943 in Orlando, Florida, and buried there		
Two (2) Half Brothers:	Kenneth Lavon (Bug) Eldridge	Born: Nov. 5, 1946	Died Jan. 6, 2016
	Charlie Ray Eldridge	Born: Nov. 7, 1947	Died:
One (1) Stepbrother:	James Leonard Hart (JL) Jr.	Born: Sept.7, 1937	Died: Dec. 27, 2004

WHEN WERE YOUR CHILDREN BORN?

| Son: | Larry Leon Eldridge | Born: Aug. 28, 1954 | Died: |
| Daughter: | Virginia Lynn Eldridge | Born: Aug. 27, 1956 | Died |

WHERE DOES YOUR FAMILY COME FROM ORIGINALLY?

The Eldridge's came from England. However, my great-grandparents moved from Dooley County, Georgia, to Colquitt County, Georgia, in the early 1900s.

SHARE A STORY THAT WAS TOLD TO YOU AS A BOY

This is a family story. My grandfather, Homer, had taken my dad, Everett (Shorty), to town with him in a horse wagon. After they arrived in town, my grandfather told my dad not to talk to anyone because they might think he was a stupid kid.

While my dad was sitting there minding his own business, a man walked up and asked him his name. Remembering what my grandfather had told him, my dad would not say a word to this man. This man offered him an apple if he would tell him his name. After a few brief moments of trying to learn his name, the man sort of said to himself out loud, "You must be stupid kid," and walked away. After my grandfather came back, my dad told him about the man trying to get him to give him his name. Then he told my grandfather, "He learned that I was stupid, and I did not even open my mouth."

YOUR EARLY DAYS

GRANDPA, WHEN IS YOUR BIRTHDAY?

My birthday is September 28, 1933.

WHERE WERE YOU BORN?

I was born in Winter Haven, Florida, shortly after the huge hurricane of September of 1933. My mother was due to have me anytime; and since we had no telephones, my dad went to fetch the doctor while my grandfather, Homer, stayed with my mother who was in labor. During their absence, I was born with the assistance of my grandfather. When the doctor and my dad came to the house, I was there to greet them—what a surprise!

HOW DID YOUR MOM PICK YOUR NAME?

My mom did not pick my name. Since my grandfather had assisted in my delivery, my mom and dad gave him the choice of naming me. He named me Homer Jackson, after himself, and Ferrell after a friend of his. That is the name on my birth certificate, Homer Jackson Ferrell Eldridge, and they nicknamed me Buddy.

WHO WAS PRESIDENT WHEN YOU WERE BORN?

Franklin D. Roosevelt was president of the United States of America when I was born. He was the thirty-first president and was only in office for about three months after I was born.

WHAT WAS YOUR CHILDHOOD HOME LIKE?

I had several childhood homes when I was growing up, and I will briefly describe each of them. The first one that I remember was in a small area of Orlando, Florida, known as Angel Belt. This is the place where my two brothers were born. We lived in a small modest home and had a lot of chickens in a large pen near the house. My dad would buy the day-old bread to feed the chickens as it was less expensive than regular chicken feed. In the bags were assorted types of cakes with icing on them, and we would pull the icing off the cakes and feed it to Uncle Gene who loved every bit of it. My brothers and I would often slip away from home to visit our lovely neighbors, the Sangsters, who were an elderly couple that raised and cross-pollinated amaryllis plants. I remember that they had an old rooster that would attack Uncle Gene and me when nobody else was around, so we had to be extra careful when visiting them. Uncle Gene would almost always pull his clothes off when he visited the Sangsters and come home naked as a jaybird. We had an old windmill in our backyard that pumped water to a storage container for future use. It was at this house that we lost our little puppy named Pat. Since this is the house where Uncle Pat was born and it was about the same time we lost our puppy, Uncle Gene called our baby brother Pat, and the nickname has been there ever since. The name Pat is not on his birth certificate.

My second home was also in Orlando, Florida, in an area called Ivanhoe. This also was a modest little home but larger than the previous one because our family had outgrown the other one. This area was a clean and quiet neighborhood with very good neighbors. One of our neighbors had large cherry trees as a shrubby and would let us eat them when they were ripe. We had to get permission prior to consuming the cherries because they belonged to the neighbors and not our family.

My third home was a temporary place where we lived until my dad could move another building on to our lot and prepare for occupation. This home was across the corner from the baseball park in Orlando, Florida, called Tinker Field and a small mom-and-pop grocery store owned by the Beasleys. They were very good to us, and we would go there to purchase candy and articles for our parents. One of the main items was ice. Back in those days, we did not have refrigerators, so we had to purchase ice and keep it in an icebox like the one in Mema's kitchen in Georgia. This would keep our food chilled, and the ice had to be replaced often to maintain a good temperature.

My fourth home was on the corner of Pine Street and Ohio Avenue on the west side of Orlando, Florida, about one mile from our third home. Daddy moved a building to this lot for us to live in while he was building our home. It was real crowded, but we managed. Daddy designed and built our new home nearly by himself as he was an excellent carpenter and was not afraid to work hard. He built this home during the year of 1940, and we lived there until December 1945, at which time we moved to Moultrie, Georgia, to a farm on Perry Road near Berlin, Georgia. Some of our family is still living on some of the property at this date.

My mother, Anna Malinda Hodge, lived with us until September 1940, at which time her and our dad were divorced. Things were pretty hectic around our house for a while. Daddy would work at the Army base during the day and would do maintenance work on some apartments near our home in the evening. Later on he started a paper route, and now he had three jobs.

Daddy would find time to do a little partying from time to time and would leave us with our granddaddy to babysit. Granddaddy would never complain but would always try to entertain us the best he could and keep us fed. Granddaddy had these little stories that he would tell us about him being a "high sheriff" and what he did during that time. He was never a sheriff as far as my history of him goes. He also had these little things he would do with his hands and some other funny sayings that I cannot remember. Daddy was divorced for about two years, and then he met our stepmother, Thelma Gertrude Hart, at a peanut boiling hosted by our uncle Clarence Mims near Sunset Community, which is south of Moultrie. After a short romance, they were married on May 30, 1942. She immediately came to live with us and did the best she could with four growing kids. Remember now, Daddy had four children at this time and no wife. At the time they were married, Betty was ten years old; I, Papa, was nine years old; Gene was five years old; and Pat was only three years old. Our stepmother had a son, James Leonard Hart Jr., who was only four years old at that time. There was only nine months and nine days difference in Pat's age and JL's age. I believe everything got off to a good start until our dad tried to discipline JL, and then things went haywire. However, we learned to tolerate this for many years, and Daddy tolerated her behavior because he had nobody else to take care of all the children.

When I was about ten years old, I tried to find something to do away from the house so I could make myself a little money. I worked as a sheet metal cleaner to start with but found employment with my grandfather washing dishes in a restaurant. I washed dishes twelve hours a day for $1 a day until he and I moved to another restaurant in the middle of Orlando, Florida. He paid me $15 per week, and I did not have to work as many hours; so that made it much better. This is when I purchased my first bicycle from Sears and Roebuck for about $29.95. I was really doing great to have a good job and a new bicycle all at the same time. Just about the time I was enjoying all these good benefits, World War II ended, and I had to quit my job to move. We did enjoy living at this home because we had a large yard to play in and nobody to disturb us. My brothers and I played cowboys and Indians a lot and rode any kind of stick we could as our horse. We had guns and ropes to go along with our horses, and we had a great time. We also had huge oak trees to climb, which was not a favorite thing to do around our parents or grandfather. They were always afraid that we were going to fall and break something, but we never did. We also had lots of friends in this area, and we enjoyed playing with them from time to time.

We had cows and pigs on our land and had to take care of them so we could have meat to eat and milk to drink. We even had a nanny goat to milk so our stepmother could have the rich milk for her ulcers. Goat's milk was supposed to be an excellent liquid for stomach ulcers.

My fifth and final home of my childhood was in Moultrie, Georgia. It was on a farm bought by my dad when he retired from the Army base in Orlando after World War II ended. We moved there in December of 1945 during our Christmas school break. My dad and I brought all our cows, pigs, and horses up to Georgia in our new truck. Dad had bought a new Chevrolet truck and built the bodies in our backyard in Florida. After we had all the animals unloaded and put away in their proper places, we cleaned the truck so he could go back to Florida to get the rest of our family. He allowed me to stay with my aunt Evie, my uncle Artie, and their ten children while he went to fetch the rest of my family. They had a good trip back to Georgia, and all arrived well and safe. My two brothers and my stepbrother rode in the back with the furniture, and my sister rode in the cab of the truck with my stepmother and dad. Once they arrived on the farm, we unloaded all the furniture and put it in our respective rooms as we had enough for everyone, although we boys had to double up for sleeping.

We had plenty of neighborhood children to play with, and we made friends very fast. All of us boys soon found us a sweetheart at school and sort of wrote notes back and forth for a long time. I could not make up my mind on who I wanted to be my sweetheart; therefore, I "played the field," as they say in school.

We worked very hard on the farm, and the chores were never done; they just kept growing as we got older. We would arise early each morning to feed the mules, horses, and cows. After they were fed, we would go to the cow pen and milk the cows. Sometimes we would pull pranks on one another while milking the cows. From time to time I would squirt milk on Aunt Betty or Uncle Gene from the cow's udder, and that would get a fiery reaction from either one of them. We had to milk the cows so we could have milk, butter, and buttermilk. We made our own butter by churning the sour milk for a long length of time either with a churn or in a glass jar, and the by-product was buttermilk. Sometimes, when we were done with our chores, Dad would let us boys go to a favorite swimming hole called Chapman's Hole. There was nothing but boys in the swimming hole, so we skinny-dipped; that is, we had nothing on but our birthday suit. Otherwise, we had no clothes on while swimming. We had some good times on the farm, and it was not all work and no play.

One thing you must know about our home in Georgia is that we had no inside plumbing whatsoever. Our bath room was a small building behind our house, and it was called an outhouse. It was about four-foot square and about seven feet tall. Inside there was a sort of bench to the back of the little house, and it had a hole cut in it so we could use the bathroom there. It was crude and was very primitive in style and stature. Since there was no indoor plumbing, it was necessary for us to have a container that we could use during the night if we needed to go to the bathroom. This container was called a slop jar, and it had a cover on it. Each morning, it was necessary for one of us to take this container out and empty it, wash it, and hang it on a post installed especially for hanging this container on it so it could drain and be ready for the next night. It was crude, but it worked for us. It was still this way when I joined the Navy in October of 1951. My sister, Aunt Betty, had an inside bathroom installed when she came to stay with my folks while her husband, Uncle Jabe Sherertz, was on a ship overseas in the Navy. We had no water heater either. Our water was heated in a reservoir on the side of our wood-burning cook stove, and we used it for washing dishes and bathing in a large tin tub. However, being the entrepreneur that I am, I made a shower for us boys to bath under during the warmer days. I put a fifty-five-gallon drum on one of our buildings and had it plumbed so we could turn on the water from inside the curtain. We would fill this drum with water at night, and the next day, it was heated by the sun; therefore, we had hot running water to bathe with. It was not much to look at, but it worked like a charm and was energy efficient as well.

My stepmother cooked everything on a wood-burning stove. Before she could cook, a fire had to be made so it would be easier for the cook to manage it when necessary. The oven was in the same place as our stoves today and had a large door in the front. Once the stove gained the temperature desired, the cook could cook anything they wanted. That was a long way from all our instant heated appliances today.

Back to the good times we were talking about before. We had horses to ride and plenty of neighborhood kids to play with; and when we grew older, we went to a lot of parties at various kids' houses. Most of the time it was supervised by adults; therefore, we couldn't get away with too much misbehaving. We went to church regularly and participated in most of the activities there. We learned at an early age that we were supposed to worship God/Jesus in a reverent way and abide by His rules in and out of church. I was a leader in our Bible sword drills and could find verses very fast. It always pleased me to do well in my church studies, and it made my family proud as well.

LIFE AS A CHILD

———•———

WHAT DID YOU LOVE MOST
ABOUT BEING A CHILD?

I guess it was being a part of a multi-child family. I always loved my siblings, and they loved me. That was a given in our family growing up. Of course, we had our little spats once in a while, but that is all part of being children. We could squabble when we wanted to, but we didn't let anybody talk about or scuffle with one of our siblings. We would all jump on them if necessary to settle the score very fast. We had a great time playing with one another, and we always had a good theme to our playing time. Like we would play cowboys a lot, and we would draw the outline of our corral and the saloon where all the cowboys went to drink and play cards. We could get very theatrical at times and even pretend to kiss our girls as they did in the movies. You see, we went to the movies a lot when we were in Orlando, so we knew how all the cowboys acted and the roles they played. Some had to be good cowboys, and some had to be bad cowboys; and that is the way we played a lot. No matter where we went, we always had our siblings to play with; and we did not have to worry about finding someone to play with away from home. However, we did have a lot of cousins to play with both in Orlando and in Moultrie.

WHAT IS ONE OF YOUR FAVORITE MEMORIES ABOUT YOUR MOM AND DAD?

I was very young when my mom and dad divorced, so I am limited on good memories of them and us being together.

However, we went to the movies a lot and were always together during the evenings for dinner. We all sat down at a large table and actually ate together because there were no televisions or hi-fi radios to listen to and no distractions other than us boys wrestling in the living room. On Sunday afternoon, we would visit my dad's brother, Uncle Quinton, who was in an orphanage in DeLand, Florida. Sometimes Dad would take us to the springs nearby, and we could swim in the very cold water. At other times, we would go visit some friends of my dad who had three invalid boys that were bedridden all the time. This would make them very happy that someone cared enough to visit them regularly.

On most Sunday evenings, Dad and Mom would take us to this new ice-cream store in Colonial Town that made a new ice cream called custard. It was so good and creamy, and of course, we all loved it.

DID YOU HAVE CHORES TO DO EACH DAY?

As long as I can remember, there were certain chores that had to be done by all of us kids in the family. We would be required to make our beds the best we could and sweep the floor of our bedroom floors to a certain point, after which our mother or stepmother would sweep it farther or pick it up. We were required to assist in tending to the animals we owned. We had cows, goats, pigs, and dogs when I was young and living in Orlando, Florida. All the animals had to be cared for prior to us having any free time for ourselves. I learned to milk the cows and goats at an early age. During the summer vacation, I would help my grandfather in the restaurant kitchen where he cooked. I started working with him when I was about eleven years old, and I made a dollar a day until he moved to a larger restaurant in the city of Orlando; and then he raised my pay to fifteen dollars a week. I thought I had struck it rich, and with that pay raise, I purchased me a large bicycle from Sears. I have also explained in the topic "What Was Your Childhood Home Like?" about the many chores we had as a farm kid.

WHAT WERE YOUR FAVORITE OR YOUR LEAST FAVORITE FOODS?

I was raised in a large family basically controlled by a disciplinarian father. We would be given a portion of food at each meal, and we would either eat it or explain why we did not. I grew up eating most anything prepared for us by my mother or my stepmother. None of us were very picky about our diet except our stepbrother, JL. I do not guess that I had a least-liked food when I was a child; however, we never had many exotic foods to select from, only the basic normal family foods.

DID YOU HAVE A FAVORITE MOVIE OR SHOW?

As previously stated, we went to many movies as a kid in Orlando, and it was especially true on Saturday mornings. Daddy would always drop us off at the movie in the morning; and we would sit there through two movies, a cartoon, a weekly serial movie, and the news portion. There would always be a cowboy movie, and we loved them as we played the part when we were at home. We had no TV or video games, and sometimes we would listen to the *Grand Ole Opry* on the radio on Saturday nights. There were several radio programs that we listened to on a regular basis. We would actually sit around in our living room and be quiet enough for everyone to hear the radio.

HOW DID YOU LIKE TO PASS THE TIME DURING A FREE AFTERNOON?

We would play in the yard at our home in Orlando as we did not have but one family near us at that time. We played cowboys and other games that we would make up as we went along. We had some large oak trees in our yard, and we would climb very high on the limbs that would hold us. We would go swimming almost every afternoon in a lake near our home in Orlando. There were always plenty of our friends there to help entertain us.

WHAT WAS THE BEST PLACE FOR YOU TO PLAY AS A KID?

As stated above, our yard was our theater and playground. It is the place that we felt most comfortable and safe from all other encroachments. We knew that our yard boundaries were the only place we could play and would not stray out of our limited area. However, we had two junkyards near us, and we would love to ramble through the old cars and play in the large trucks stored there. A junkyard is a place where businesses stored wrecked or disabled vehicles and sold their replacement parts to automobile repair garages. It was a place that we could get out of the environment and be by ourselves when we wanted to. Sometimes we would take our girlfriends to these wrecks and play different games.

SCHOOL DAYS

GRANDPA, DO YOU REMEMBER WHEN YOU WERE A SCHOOLBOY?

Yes, I do remember when I was a schoolboy. I am old, but I am not senile yet; and it has not been that long ago that I was a little boy like you and did most of the same things that you do. I did not get away with some of the stuff you do and was chastised by my father for doing some of those things. My dad was very disciplined.

WHERE WAS YOUR FIRST SCHOOL?

My first school was Concord Grammar School in Orlando, Florida, which was located on Colonial Drive or Highway 50. The school has been torn down, but my memories of that school still linger in my mind. During my first year at this school, I contacted pneumonia and was sick a great deal; therefore, I failed the first grade and had to repeat my first year.

WHO WAS YOUR BEST TEACHER?

In my first school I cannot remember a single teacher that stands out in my mind as being real supportive of me, nor do I remember any of their names; however, that was in 1938 and 1939, and I was only six years old at that time.

However, as times went on and I went through many different grades throughout my educational experience, I had many teachers that stand out in my mind, of which some had more impact on me than others.

My seventh-grade teacher in Berlin Grammar School was Mr. Jesse Weeks; he was a big bald-headed man with several fingers missing from one hand. He was also the principal of the school. He taught us math as if we were clerks in a store or as if we were farmers conducting business with the outside world, and this impressed me from the start.

Another teacher that stands out in my mind was my physics teacher, Mr. Ike Aultman, who was also a football coach. He talked about football more than he talked about physics, and maybe that is the reason he passed everyone in his classes. However, my most favorite teacher of all was Mr. C. T. Haralson, my high school industrial arts instructor. He taught us the correct way to use all carpentry tools, both manual and electric. We manufactured many things of laminated wood and used the turn lathe to make a design in them. I still have some of the items I made in 1950 and 1951. Mr. Haralson had no use of his legs, but he made up for it with strength in his arms. He could motivate on his crutches better than some could on their legs. He was a great inspiration to me and many other kids.

In college I had some good teachers as well, and most of them were very professional in their behavior and mannerisms. I do not remember his name, but my zoology professor taught us all the things we needed to know; and most of it was in the laboratory where we dissected frog and pigs. He taught us that pigs' organs were in the same location and had the same functions as humans. This was one of my most interesting classes in college.

WHAT WERE YOUR FAVORITE AND LEAST FAVORITE SUBJECTS?

I enjoyed many of the subjects taught to me during my educational experience; however, my science and biology classes were more interesting than some of the others. I learned from hands-on experience, and a lot of it was in the laboratory. However, my best of all classes was my industrial arts woodwork classes; this is where I learned all about working with wood and the use of the tools of the trade. I still use that training today as I perform my construction work.

My least-liked class had to be Latin. I could not get the hang of all the conversion from Latin to English, and that bothered me very much. I only took the class because it was a prerequisite to becoming a doctor, and that was my goal in life at one time.

DID YOU GO TO COLLEGE?
WHAT DID YOU STUDY?

Yes, I went to a junior college and took courses that would qualify me to become a doctor of some kind. I did very well in college by studying very long and hard. I made much better grades in college than I did in high school because I had more time to study and had a much better objective in life. I had an old reel recorder that I carried to class and recorded all actions so I could study better when alone. I had to drive many miles to night classes for the subjects needed for my curriculum. I started going to college in Palatka, Florida, for some subjects and then went to classes in the old Orange Park High School for others and ended up in Saint Augustine, Florida, for a math class. When they opened a junior college in Jacksonville, Florida, I transferred to it and studied for another year or so. However, all my time away from Mema, Larry, and Lynn did not go well with my family; so I stopped going to college after earning in excess of forty-two semester hours. By quitting college, all was not wasted since the time spent in college helped me tremendously in my naval career and in my federal government job as well. No education will go to waste if you want to use it wisely.

WHAT KIND OF ACTIVITIES WERE YOU INVOLVED IN THROUGHOUT YOUR SCHOOL YEARS?

I was involved in a lot of sports in grammar school and in high school but not any structured sports. One fall, I practiced for the Moultrie High Football Team; however, when it came time to work on the farm, my father made me quit football practice and come to work on the farm. That was the end of my football career.

I did study wood craftsmanship for four years in high school. I made many pieces of articles out of wood, and I learned to use all the hand and power tools of the carpenter trade. I have used this knowledge to follow the trade throughout my career in building and remodeling homes and reroofing.

ANIMAL FRIENDS

GRANDPA, DID YOU TAKE CARE OF ANIMALS WHEN YOU WERE GROWING UP?

As you have read prior to this event, I have owned and taken care of many kinds of animals. I have always been sympathetic to animals as they depend on humans to care for them and see to their well-being and needs. As pets, I have had many dogs, cats, horses, cows, pigs, and goats. All these animals have a unique and different need for care than the other. We had to provide the type of food for each of them that they were accustomed to. The horses, cows, and goats can share the same food with only slight changes according to their basic demands. Pigs require other types of food, and the cats and dogs require their kind of food manufactured for them according to their requirements or sometimes food from the human table.

This is a short story about how much I cared about animals. One day as I was walking home from work, I saw a small baby goat entangled in some wire near an old service station. Seeing that this small goat was in trouble, I asked the owner if he wanted to get rid of this goat. He said that he would sell it to me if I wanted it. I had just been paid, so I bought the small goat for the same amount of money that I had been paid ($6); and I carried this goat all the way home in my arms, which was about two miles. My family could not believe that I had done such a thing. I can't remember how long we kept the goat, but at least it was out of trouble and in a safe place. I was about nine or ten years old at that time.

WHAT PETS DID YOU HAVE AS A CHILD? WHAT WERE THEIR NAMES?

We have had many dogs and cats during our lifetime, and it would be difficult to name all of them; however, below is a list of animals and their names as best as I can recollect:

A male bulldog puppy (Chum)

A male coyote-breed dog (Butch)

A male cocker spaniel (Lucky)

A female cocker spaniel (Frisky)

A female pica poo (Lady)

A female cat (Mittens)

A male Cuban cat (Gato)

A female cat (Muffin)

A riding horse (Cherry)

A riding horse (Lady)

A pet pig (Spotted Sausage)

A pet goat (Billy)

A female chihuahua (Tangy)

A male beagle (Henry)

A male Labrador

A male cat (Britches)

IF YOU COULD'VE HAD ANY KIND OF PET AS A KID, WHAT WOULD YOU HAVE CHOSEN?

It is hard to determine which kind of animal I would have chosen; however, I believe it would be a dog, an outside dog. I also love to ride horses, and it was always good to have one to ride places when I was a small kid. It is fun to be all by yourself on a horse out there in the wide-open spaces and ride places you do not normally go on foot. One gets attached to an animal, and sometimes it is difficult to let them go when they die because they are like part of the family. Some animals we kept for seventeen to nineteen years and watched them do so many things that were almost human in action. Mema and I have several buried on the farm that we loved dearly, and they are buried in a special box or container made especially for them.

DID YOU LET YOUR CHILDREN HAVE PETS?

Yes, I encouraged Larry and Lynn to have animals; however, Mema and I always picked out puppies. We had two puppies while living in Hyde Park but gave them away when it became too much to care for them. Having pets normally gave the children a better responsibility if they did their chores correctly. It is good to have something that gives one responsibilities, and it also promotes discipline. It makes one very sad when you lose a pet that you have had for a long time because they become part of the family and can get expensive if taken care of correctly. They also had a horse that their grandfather, Wheeler Norman, kept on the farm for them. They both loved to ride, and it gave them a satisfaction to learn to ride and control a horse. Normally, caring for a horse is a little more involved than caring for a cat or a dog; however, they can be much more fun.

TIME FOR EVERYTHING

—————•————•————

WHAT IS YOUR FAVORITE SEASON
OF THE YEAR, GRANDPA?

I guess I would choose spring time as my favorite time of the year. Mema and I sat on our porch many times in the early spring and were amazed at the beauty and wonders of the Lord's creation (not the Big Bang one either). We could see the actual beauty of the world as God created it. All the animals are scurrying around to find food after a lean winter and trying to find a mate to raise their offspring with. Then, together, they will select a place to build a nest or home for themselves according to their own wishes. Some build homes on the open dirt, some build their homes in the trees, some build their homes in the bushes, and some make holes in the ground. During this time, beauty breaks out all over the countryside and all the trees and bushes put on new growth to beautify the countryside and make everything beautiful. However, in the fall, everything is decaying, dying off for the winter, or just going dormant. The spring makes everyone more cheerful as new life starts to be evident and there is a big bustle in the air. People are even different in the spring than they are in the fall or winter except at Christmas, then everyone is so nice and polite.

DID YOU VISIT YOUR HOMETOWN LATER? HOW HAD IT CHANGED?

After living in Georgia for several years, in 1952, we did go back to Orlando for a visit when I was home on leave from the Navy. Our old home and the immediate area had not changed very much. Our uncle and aunt Yearwood still lived in the same place across the street from our old home. However, a few years later, I returned for a visit, and many changes had taken place. They had removed all the orange trees and built stores and houses where our cow pasture was previously located. All our old neighbors had moved, and lots of others had moved in and taken over. A lot of them looked like hoodlums, and it was a high-crime area; however, when we lived there, it was a quiet, peaceful, and safe community. Now there are freeways over the spot where our home was built.

WHAT WAS THE STROLL DOWN MEMORY LANE LIKE?

It was devastating to see our great neighborhood taken over by hoodlums and turned into a high-crime area. It was much more emotional to see that they had replaced our neighborhood with a freeway and off-ramps. There was nothing there to remind us that we ever lived in the area. None of the old homes or neighbors were there nor were any of our favorite play areas left standing. At one time, we had a new home built by my father, and it was the nicest home in the area. We had an extraordinary yard to play in and a peaceful one. All the huge oak trees that we climbed were destroyed and removed. It was a desolate place now.

WHAT YEARS OF YOUR CHILDHOOD ARE MOST DEAR TO YOU?

That is a difficult question since I had such a great childhood both in Orlando, Florida, and in Colquitt County, Georgia. In Florida, I was raised from birth to twelve years old and enjoyed most all of it. We did not have very many chores except the ones around the house and the area around the yard. We did most anything we wanted as long as we were not bad to one another and remained civil about our actions. We had some large oak trees that were about a hundred feet high, and we would even climb to the top of them until our parents caught us and made us get back down on the ground. I had a tremendous amount of friends that I could play with all over the neighborhood, and lots of them were girls, which I liked a lot. There were two old junkyards (this is a place where they stored old wrecked cars and trucks) in our neighborhood in which we could rummage through the cars and trucks just to see what we could find to play with. It was a lot of fun, and we enjoyed that very much, especially when the girls were with us.

Sometimes I look back and wonder where my childhood actually stopped. During my summer vacations, I started working with my grandfather in the restaurant where he was a cook when I was almost ten. I earned a dollar ($1) a day for the first summer. The next summer we changed jobs and started working at another restaurant. There I made fifteen dollars ($15) a week and worked long hours. I washed dishes for about ten to twelve hours a day, and that was a lot of dishes. I also have a lot of fond childhood memories in Georgia; however, a lot of our time there was either working or going to school. On weekends, mostly Sundays, we would either visit our relatives or they would come visit us. We children would sit around and listen to the adults tell stories of the past or some silly family story. We always enjoyed those evenings, but the children were not allowed to join in on many of the conversations as we were supposed to "be seen and not heard," as the story goes. So to answer the question, I guess my first twelve years were most precious to me since I was able to act as a child most of the time.

WHEN DID YOU FIRST THINK
ABOUT YOUR FUTURE?

In high school, I took the basic courses to allow me to go to college; however, I had a feeling that I would never make it since there were too many kids for my dad to afford me going to college. I guess I first got serious about my future when I saw so many of my cousins not being able to read nor write as they should and always working very hard for someone else. They just did not appear to be getting anyplace in life where they could be independent; however, they depended on someone else to assist them or help them in life. Also, my last year in high school was a tough one since my father kept us from starting school on schedule like most of the other kids. He made us handpick all his cotton, which was fifty acres. I definitely knew that I did not want to be a farmer the rest of my life, so I started looking elsewhere for a job. I was hired as a mechanic's helper at the old Spence Field Airbase when I graduated from high school in 1951. To be truthful, I still did not have any idea what occupation I was going to pursue; however, I did know that I wanted to get away from the farm. That is when I decided to join the Navy with some friends of mine, and that is where it all began. As they say, "the rest is history."

GREAT OUTDOORS

WHEN YOU PLAYED AS A CHILD, WHAT WAS YOUR FAVORITE OUTDOOR ACTIVITY?

I guess my favorite activity was chasing the little girls in my neighborhood. They were all so cute, and they liked for me to chase them. I knew this because they would slow down when I got tired of running and let me catch them. The prize was, I got to kiss them in front of all the others, and that made the other boys jealous. I would go over to my girl cousin's house and play several games that we could all participate in. We would play tag-you-are-it, dodgeball, "red rover, red rover send (a name of a person) on over," hide-and-seek, and toss the ball over the house. This game is when we would toss a softball or another ball over the house. When you caught it, you would run to the other side and throw it at someone. When you hit them, they became part of your team. Just clean, fun games are all we played.

CAN YOU RECALL THE LANDSCAPE THAT SURROUNDED YOU AS A CHILD?

My memory is still so vivid about the landscape around my old home in Florida. We had a lot of orange trees and two enormous oak trees. Our yard was previously an orange grove prior to Daddy clearing enough land to build our home. We had a small house on our property that we lived in until Daddy completed our home enough that we could live in it. It was really crowded because there was Daddy,

Mother, Betty, Gene, Pat, Granddaddy, and me in that small temporary home. We had our cow pen and hog pen across the road so it would not be too smelly. We were not too far from a large beautiful lake that we swam in a lot. We would walk down to the lake with our parents and swim until dark; we enjoyed this time of day together. I can remember where our neighbors lived and my grandparents and all my other relatives in the neighborhood. In my mind, I can see their homes and can tell you what was in each room. It was in that neighborhood that I saw my grandfather last. He passed away a few days later, and it was a sad time for us as he would let us help him feed his chickens and work around the yard.

DID YOU EVER MAKE A FORT IN THE WOODS? A TRAIL IN THE MEADOW? A TREE HOUSE?

Yes, we did all the above. We would make a fort in the automobile junkyard so we could hide from the other kids that we did not want to play with. We also had trails in the woods both in Florida and in Georgia. It seemed that we just like to make trails in the tall grass and weeds. We would make different patterns and just made a game out of this adventure. On the farm we had a lot more brushland to make trails in than in Florida. In Georgia there were streams running through our farm, so we also had a place to drink water from; and it was so cool and refreshing. It was icy cold and always tasted so good. We had one tree in Florida that we built a tree house in; it was a large oak tree that was very tall. We would build it so high that most of the kids were afraid to climb up in it, and then we would have our privacy. In Georgia we did not have time enough to build a tree house nor play in one as we worked most of the afternoons and were too busy to play. However, we did have a place that we went to swing into a water hole in the afternoons after work was finished. It was nothing but boys, and we would take our clothes off and swim in our "birthday" suits; otherwise, we were naked to the skin. My cousins and some of the other neighborhood kids would join us most of the time. No girls were allowed.

IF YOU COULD SHOW ME ONE SPECIAL PLACE IN NATURE, WHERE WOULD IT BE?

I do not believe that it would a particular one spot. It would have to be the little stream that we drank from and the washing hole in the creek near the house. These were two special places to us because it provided us a sense of being on our own and just enjoying nature's gift to us. Neither place was man-made, and that appealed to us a lot. These were areas that the Lord had made, and we enjoyed the unmolested places in the wild and also enjoyed their natural beauty. Most children never see a place like this and do not understand why we love the wilderness so much. One never wants to leave it for another crowded area like the small neighborhoods that we have lived in; some of them are so crowded and full of mean kids and angry adults. You can remember as a child when you came to the farm to visit Mema and me and how much more you enjoyed the wide-open spaces on the farm and all the fishing places you fished from. You always hated to leave the farm and go back to the crowded city. Gramps was the same way when he was a small boy. When he went back to school, he would daydream about his grandpa and the farm instead of studying as he should have. When you boys were returning home from visiting us in Georgia, you would say, "Florida stinks," when you crossed the line.

FAITH TRADITIONS

DID YOUR FAMILY GO TO CHURCH WHEN YOU WERE A BOY?

Yes, my family has always gone to church as long as I can remember. We were raised in a Southern Baptist church in Orlando, Florida; and when we moved to Georgia, we joined a Southern Baptist church in Berlin, Georgia, and went regularly. As children, we participated in Sunday school and had Bible sword drills a lot. A sword drill is when someone calls out a verse in the Bible and you see who can find it the fastest and announce it. This gives one lots of practice on learning the books of the Bible. I went to church regularly up until I joined the Navy. In the Navy they also have churches, known as chapels, for Bible believers to attend. I attended our Navy church and even joined the choir in the church. Papa has always been a God believer, and I know that God looks after His people no matter what circumstances or difficulties arise. It is a known fact that when you are in church, you are not doing evil to others nor to yourself.

WHAT WAS YOUR FAVORITE PRAYER FOR BEDTIME AND MEALTIME?

I guess one of the earlier prayers that we were taught in Sunday school and by our parents was a short prayer that a lot of children say, "Now I lay me down to sleep, I pray Thee Lord my soul to keep. If I die before I wake, hope the Lord my soul will take, amen." It is a simple prayer and easy to learn, and it asks the Lord to be with you even through death. One cannot ask for any more than that. Prayer is not for a lot of words; it is the sincere desire from the heart directed to God our Father. We as children would take turns saying the mealtime blessing, just as you boys always did. The most common one we would say was short and simple and easy to learn: "God is great, God is good, and we thank him for this food, amen."

WHAT WAS YOUR FAVORITE VERSE OR MEMORY FROM CHURCH?

One of the first verses I learned in school was John 3:16, so I guess that would be one of my favorites. I was in the third grade in Central Grammar School in Orlando, Florida; and they actually taught us Bible verses. I received my first New Testament in that grade after I learned the first chapter of John. However, I do have many favorite verses in the Bible, and it is difficult to say which is the most favorite. As you get older and read more of the Bible and hear the God-given men preach, you tend to pick out verses that mean a lot more to you and can symbolize many things within your life. Each one brings a different highlight to your heart and just warms your soul when you either read the verse or think of it during the day.

My favorite memory of church was the night that Mema and I joined Sardis Primitive Baptist Church on May 26, 1959. Both of us were inspired by the Lord to join and become more active in our church, and we did. We have many fond memories of the members that have gone to be with the Lord from our church. Each of them had a small amount of helping us mold our lives and becoming better members and better people. It goes without saying that the Lord had more to do with this than the members or our families; however, He inspired them to show us the way to act and conduct ourselves in church, especially while in conference each month. Sardis Church ordained me as a deacon on May 31, 1970. Some other favorite memories in church were while in Orlando, Florida. During Christmas time, my father would be instrumental in providing many children with toys. Without this act of kindness, many children would get nothing for Christmas. He would also give the children nuts and candy as well. I always enjoyed seeing this act of kindness portrayed by my father.

WHAT IS YOUR PRAYER FOR ME, GRANDPA?

I guess my prayer for you is that God would protect you from harm and keep you safe at all times. It would also be that you succeed in whatever you delight to do. Also, that you will be true to our Lord, your country, your family, and most of all, to yourself. One can easily lie to others; however, you will never be able to lie to God or yourself; your conscious will always get the best of you if you try to do so. My additional prayer is that you will be a happy person and a delightful person to work with and be associated with.

Psalm 119:1–8 says a great deal about guidance, "¹Blessed are the undefined in the way, who walk in the law of the Lord. ²Blessed are they that keep his testimonies, and that seek him with the whole heart. ³They also do no iniquity; they walk in his ways. ⁴Thou hast commanded us to keep thy precepts diligently. ⁵O that my ways were directed to keep thy statutes! ⁶Then shall I not be ashamed, when I have respect unto all thy commandments. ⁷I will praise thee with uprightness of heart, when I shall have learned thy righteous judgments. ⁸I will keep thy statutes: O forsake me not utterly."

My prayer of thanks for you being in life would be something like, "Thank you, Lord, for bringing my children (and spouses), grandchildren (and spouses), and great-grandchildren (and spouses) into my life. Help me to guide them and teach them through example to lead lives of wisdom and strong, loving faith. Please let them learn to serve you always in thought and deed. And remind me, Lord, to always be there for my family as you are always there for me. Amen." Also remember one thing, something said (either good or evil) cannot be retracted. Think before you say anything to someone you love. First Peter 3:10 says, "For he that will love life, and see good days, let him refrain his tongue from evil, and his lips that they speak no guile." The Lord loves a cheerful and truthful person.

GOOD TIMES

———•———

TELL ME ABOUT A TIME WHEN YOU WERE REALLY HAPPY

I am too old now to single out a one time that I was really happy. There are many times in my life that I was overjoyed with happiness. Like when Mema and I were married; when we learned that Mema was expecting our child; when each of our children were born and were healthy and strong; when Gramps and Grammy were married; when Diana and Lisa were born; when they both were married; and very top on the list is when each of our four boys, Christopher (Punkin), Bradley, Cameron, and Blake, were born. Mema and I were there and welcomed each of you into our family, and we knew that each of you would bring us much love and joy. So you see, one cannot pick a single time when we were any happier than another time that brought us lots of joy and happiness. Each of you boys have given us many happy times and continue to do so as we get older. As most of you know, it doesn't take much to make us old folks happy or to make us smile at some little things that our boys do or say from time to time.

WHAT HOBBIES OR ACTIVITIES HAVE BROUGHT YOU JOY OVER THE YEARS?

I had many hobbies over the years that brought me great joy and satisfaction. I guess my first hobby was chasing those little girls in my neighborhood in Orlando many years ago. We had a large yard and the little girls would come over and we would play many games. I would explain some of them to you, but you may get into trouble; so I will just let you learn from your own experiences. As a high school student, I worked with wood a lot and manufactured many items for my family and myself. I made notebooks, lamps, bowls, bookcases, and other things of interest. I pursued this hobby after I joined the Navy as I worked in the hobby shop as an instructor in woodwork. I loved to ride horses as a hobby as well, and that gave me a lot of joy just being on the back of a horse riding as fast as I could through the fields and down the road. Back then there were dirt roads in our community instead of all paved roads. I have hunted coins with my brothers in many places around Orange Park and Moultrie and have found lots of different kinds of coins; however, I found nothing very rare. We would shoot (run our machines) in schoolyards, church-yards, and any place that people gathered for recreation or fun. I also collected coins from different countries and from different government mints. I have collected some coins for you boys in the past. And maybe one day they will be worth lots of money for you, or maybe you will just keep them as a memento from Mema and me.

SHARE WITH ME A STORY FROM YOUR LIFE THAT STILL MAKES YOU LAUGH

There are many stories in my life that make me laugh when I am reminded of them. Some stories involve my brothers and sister, and some involved other family members. I remember once when my stepmother was real ill and lying in her bed hardly able to move, I brought a large dead bug into her room. When she was not looking, I placed the large dead bug on her pillow so she could see it when she turned her head. When she saw that large dead bug lying on her pillow, she immediately started screaming and jumped out of her bed as if she was not sick at all. You guessed it, I sure received a good spanking for disturbing and scaring her so badly. However, I cured her from her near-death experience. You can read some other stories in another writing of mine called *Short Stories by Homer Eldridge*.

WHAT DO YOU THINK IS THE
KEY TO HAPPINESS?

I guess that different things make different people happy. What satisfies one person may not necessarily satisfy others. Most of my life I have been happy because I was with the people that I wanted to be with, and we enjoyed basically the same activities or events. The environment in which one lives has a lot to do with them being satisfied or not satisfied in most situations.

I have never particularly enjoyed confrontations with anyone, especially my family. One had to live in the same home and stay around the same people within a family, and harmony and compromise is always the best solution for all concerned.

I guess love is the key ingredient to happiness in most any situations involving human beings and their actions in an involvement. If you like to make someone happy and enjoy their company, you tend to tolerate more of their actions and their behavior. In some instances, you tend to overlook some of the things they do or say and just go with the flow, so to speak.

TAKE ME OUT TO
THE BALL GAME

———————•———————

WHAT GAMES DID YOU AND
YOUR FRIENDS PLAY?

When I was a very young boy, we did not have all the technology that you have today. A lot of our toys were handmade by us or one of our friends. We did not have any puzzles or fancy store-bought games, no cards or any fancy stuff. We played a lot of different games with our friends and cousins that lived in our neighborhood. Some of our games were played with a "make believe" stick that was ridden like a horse or a small stick that was used as a pistol. We played a lot of cowboys and Indians as seen in the movies of our day. Our "horse" was a long stick that we rode straddle of with a string tied to one end as a bridle. It is amazing what one can do with a "stick horse." We could make it run fast or slow, we could make it do tricks, and then we could make it rear up and buck us off. Of course, we would have to make all those funny noises like a horse on the trail. We would ride that stick all over the yard and pretend to do all sorts of things. One thing about a stick horse was that you did not have to feed it when you finished riding at the end of the day nor did you have to wipe him down. As previously stated, we played all types of ball games that involved one or two players or many players. On weekends, we would gather a few boys and play baseball with the neighboring kids also.

DID YOU HAVE A FAVORITE TOY?

When we were living in Orlando, my brother Gene and I had a fire truck that we pedaled as we rode many miles on an old abandoned sidewalk near our home. Mostly he would ride on the back steps and I would pedal; and then we would switch to let me ride on the back. Since I was much larger than Gene, he could not pedal me as fast as I pedaled him; however, it was a lot of fun.

We would make swings out of ropes tied to a tree limb, and that would be fun for a while; but it did not last very long. Daddy was afraid that we would hang one another, so he made us take our swing down. In Georgia I made a toy from an old tobacco stick by nailing a used Prince Albert tobacco can to the end of it. We would then find us a small round metal ring about six or eight inches in diameter. We would fold the two sides of the can so we could "cup" the ring and give it better direction. We would take the stick in our hand and roll the ring all over the yard, or sometimes we would roll it for about a half mile up to our cousin's house. You would be surprised how much fun one could have with the ring and stick. We would see who could do the most tricks with our ring and stick and see who could roll the fastest. Another toy we made was a "pull tractor." We would take an empty thread spool and notch the ends for better pulling power. We would take a rubber band, a crayon, and a pencil to finish the job. Put the crayon on one side and the pencil on the other side. Take a rubber band, and put it around the crayon on one side and the pencil on the other side. Twist the pencil to make the rubber band tight and then let it go and see whose "tractor" could pull the best. It did not take an expensive toy to make us happy. We were together, and that was what mattered to us.

AS YOUR CHILDREN GREW UP, WHAT GAMES DID YOU PLAY WITH THEM?

We had many games that we played together while we were in Georgia and when we were in Florida. They had a horse when they were very young, and it remained on the farm with Great-Great-Grandpa Norman. He and Uncle Lincoln cared for it while we were away. We would also play the "doodlebug" game while traveling to and from Florida and Georgia. Before the Interstate Highway I-10 and I-75, we had to travel through the small towns; and it took a long time to get to Grandma's, so we had to make the best of our time together.

We played football some, but there were never enough to have a team; so we did it just like Cameron and I did it: we just threw it to one another for fun. When Gramps was a small boy, he would hunt with his grandpa Norman and his uncles, Mema's brothers. Papa was normally studying his college lessons or working on the house for our family or performing duty with the Air Force or Naval reserves. I must confess that I did not play with my children as I should have; however, Papa worked all the time to help out with our expenses and to purchase additional things for our family. I held two jobs most of my adult life even when Mema and I were in California.

DO YOU HAVE FOND MEMORY OF ATTENDING OR PARTICIPATING IN A SPORT EVENT?

When I was a teenager, a group of my neighbors and I would go to different communities and play baseball on Sunday afternoon. This event was called sandlot baseball. It was a lot of fun, and we had a great time just letting the steam off. Our team was very good and our pitcher, Enos Flowers, was my neighbor on Perry Road near Grandpa Eldridge's old home. He later lost both legs in an accident. Although he was a very active man for the remainder of his life, he died in February of 2013. We always kept in contact with each other and visited when we had a chance to do so.

I went out for football training in my senior year of high school and practiced every day during the spring training. As it came closer for me to actually playing a game, my father stopped me from play-ing. I had too many chores at home to play any sport that would take me away from my chores. I really enjoyed suiting up for practice and actually getting out there and beating up on some of the other guys. It was a great way of taking my frustration out on them than an individual.

WHAT GAME DO YOU HOPE I LEARN?

I hope that all my boys will compete in some type of sport and enjoy it as much as I did in my short time of practicing football. I know all of you have the potential of playing whatever you want and doing it well. I have observed all of you play various sports in your younger years, and each of you had the desire to win at each one of them. As I write these notes to you, you have already had much better opportunities to play sports than I did in my entire life. Also, you have had the great support of your families that were willing to take you to practice and to the games and other functions. All of you have been blessed greatly.

Christopher (Punkin) has played several sports and appeared to enjoy most of them until he got into his "watching TV" mode and playing the DS. At one time, he was good at soccer, basketball, and T-ball when he wanted to play. It was just a matter of desire on his part. Punkin also liked martial arts a lot and seemed to enjoy that for a while. His forte was sketching as he was outstanding at this adventure. Mema and Papa have saved many of his drawings over the years and enjoy them very much.

Bradley tried all the sports as well and did well in T-ball, soccer, and basketball. He really had a desire to win and was a good hustler on the court and on the field. When Bradley was about six or seven years old, he could throw a wicked pass, and it was on the mark most every time. He and I tossed the ball many times together. He also loved flag football and was very good at throwing, catching, and running. Best of all, he was a leader on and off the field no matter which sport he was playing. He was a great wrestler as well and won many of his bouts. We also watched him play football in the county league, and he also did well in this adventure. He would play one position on offense and another position on defense, and he was good at either position. The coaches loved his competitive attitude.

Cameron appeared to be the most versatile one in all sports and was good at all of them. He had a determination to succeed on the court and on the field. I know that he and I played football a lot, and he could throw a very good pass and could kick well also. Cameron was the one that wanted to try anything that was exciting and energy burning; he could never stay still and was always moving. Good or bad, he was moving. He and I played basketball by ourselves many times just to practice and make him better. I believe that his calling was lacrosse. He loved to get in the game and rough the other boys up; sometimes he would get penalized, but he kept on going. He was just like his mother when she was playing co-ed soccer. She loved to level the big boys, and that was embarrassing to them for a girl to outfox them on a play. Cameron is also very good at football.

Blake always wanted to win regardless of what the score was or who he was playing. It always seemed exuberating for him to achieve a goal in soccer or in basketball. Blake liked to race his car at the annual Boy Scout Soap Box Derby and would be ecstatic when his car even came close to winning. Sometimes his car was the best of all the boys, especially the time Punkin let him borrow his in 2013. Punkin was a Cub Scout and could not race because he had advanced to the next level of scouting. That was a very honorable gesture for Punkin. It also made him proud that Blake won because he always thought Blake was his best pick, although he loved all others as well.

However, we must all realize that any game or sport is not all about winning; it is playing your best and in a fair and sportsmanlike manner. Many people are better at some things than others, and that is what competition is all about: doing your best in a professional manner and taking the breaks as they come your way. Being a good sport is always better than being a gloating winner, and nobody likes one of those types. Just be good, kind, and polite to other people as you would want them to be to you. It is a proven fact that at some times, opportunities come your way when you least expect them, and you must take advantage of that moment.

I always enjoyed playing with my boys and doing whatever they wanted to do. I could participate in any sport because I had done it before in some form. I did the same thing with your mothers when they were young and full of energy. Most of the time when we went camping, I would be the one to take them to the beach or go to the wading pool and just sit with them while they played and did whatever they liked to do. They would do the same thing you boys do when you want me to see you perform. They would yell, "Papa, look what I can do!" Of course I would act amazed at their performance as I always do with you boys. I may have seen it a thousand times, but it was always another great performance for Papa.

THE GIFT OF FRIENDSHIP

DID YOU HAVE A BEST FRIEND GROWING UP?

Yes, I had lots of good friends when I was growing up in Florida and in Georgia. The boys that were our neighbors in Orlando were very close to us, and we played a lot during our "out of school" times. They went to the same church we did, so we spent a lot of time together. Myron was Aunt Betty's age, and Eddie was my age; and we were in the same school and rode the same bus to and from school each morning and each afternoon. However, when we moved from Orlando, I lost contact with them and have not seen them since that move in 1945.

After moving to Georgia, I made friends with lots of people, but some were better than others. In 1945 I was introduced to some classmates in Berlin Georgia Grammar School and have remained friends with them until this present day; however, a lot of my friends that I played with and went to Boy Scouts with have passed away. One particular man was Mema's cousin on the May side of the family, Earl Chitty. We were good friends in grammar school and high school and eventually worked together at Moody Air Force Base and the Naval Air Station. He was an aircraft electrician, and I was an aircraft jet engine mechanic until I was promoted to an office job. He and his wife lived with Mema and me until he could purchase a home near us in Hyde Park subdivision in Duval County, Florida. He and I also carpooled together for years at Moody and the Naval Air Station.

While stationed at Miramar Naval Station, I met a sailor named Jim Swanson. I had heard that his wife was giving birth to their first child, and he had to stand duty that day. I volunteered to stand his duty so he could be with his wife at this special time. He was surprised that I did not want any pay as I could have received $20 for that duty, and that was a lot of money in 1952. After she gave birth and all was settled at home, they invited me to dinner as a special treat for doing Jim's duty. We have been friends from that time until his death on April 21, 2006. The family thought so highly of me that they nicknamed their grandson after me, Budric, with the blessings of their daughter, Debra. After I came from my deployment in Alaska, they assisted me in choosing our first apartment before Mema came to Escondido. They were always there to support us when we needed it, and Earlene had great parents as well, the Zickefooses. We still correspond with Jim's wife, Earlene, and Debra through e-mails and a telephone calls once in a while. Good friends are hard to find.

WERE YOU SHY OR OUTGOING? SERIOUS OR FUNNY?

I was not as outgoing as a youngster as I am now. I was never an introvert or anything; however, I just did not put myself on to anyone voluntarily. I became more aggressive as I got older as I had to participate in my class discussions or make a bad grade for not doing so. I guess one would say that while in high school, I was sort of a "down the middle" type of guy. I would fraternize with both the girls and the boys; however, I liked the girls better. Earl Chitty and I would go to dances at the high school gym and take different girls on occasions. After I joined the Navy, I became more outgoing because of living with all these guys from all over the United States. It seemed that each state had its own different language or dialogue or just the way they expressed themselves and their accent. One might say that I have always been sort of a clown in the family. That is one of the ways that I could interact with the crowd. I had always wanted to make people laugh and be friendly with them, and one way a person can penetrate a group a people is to make them laugh. I have always been able to retort back at people with something funny and sort of enjoy the atmosphere with one another. When my siblings and in-laws are together, we have a wonderful time making jokes and telling funny tidbits about one another. We also get a lot of jabs at one another about some of the things that we did or things that happened to us growing up.

WHAT QUALITY DO YOU THINK IS MOST IMPORTANT IN A FRIEND?

It is very difficult to say what quality one looks for in a friend as I have been wrong on several occasions. You definitely want someone that you can trust with your possessions and someone that you can relate stories to without fear that they will misquote you or incite trouble for you. I normally wanted to be around someone that showed some type of God-fearing attitude and one that did not drink, use drugs, use profane words, or use vulgar words of any kind. Our vocabulary should be that we should not depend on vulgar or ugly words to express ourselves alone or in public. I believe that being nice to others shows that one is considerate and passionate to others and one can have a better relationship than with a questionable person. Be you, and you will have many friends that will want to be with and around you in most circumstances and not be an embarrassment to anyone. God gives us the ability to think and make reasonable judgments, and we should use that talent. Do not be a brag or a "know it all" person. You have nothing that was not given to you by God and with his blessings. Read Matthew 25:14–30 and see what God does to those that waste their talents on foolish things.

SHARE A STORY ABOUT A GOOD TIME WITH FRIENDS

Other than my immediate family, my siblings are my best friends. I have shared so many good times, sorrowful times, and delightful times with them throughout my many years of living with and associating with them and their spouses.

Aunt Betty and her husband, Jack; Uncle Gene and his wife, Mary; Uncle Pat and his wife, Clarice; and Mema and I went on a cruise together. We were all away from our immediate families, our work, and all other obligations; this meant that we could concentrate on having fun together, and that we did. Our cruise was not near long enough for any of us, but it was great to have the comradery that we had. It seemed that everything we did was funny to the others as we ate and just browsed the ship with one another. We had a great time during the meals and were the center of attraction to the other passengers as they watched us in awe. The waiter was great; and after the first meal or two, he knew exactly what each of us wanted. The most notable thing was that Aunt Clarice always received a second dessert no matter what it was.

It was good that we chose the time we did to go on a cruise because, shortly thereafter, things started happening to one or another family member health-wise. We had never been on a cruise together but had been on vacation together on several occasions. We always had a great time and enjoyed one another very much. It is great to have siblings and in-laws that you can enjoy being around.

TELL ME ABOUT GRANDMA

GRANDPA, DO YOU REMEMBER WHEN YOU FIRST MET GRANDMA?

Yes, I remember very much the first time I met your grandma, Mema. I was dating her pretty cousin at the time, and they had arranged for Mema to go with another young man from the neighborhood. It turned out that Mema and I talked much more than I talked to my date; and for some unknown reason, she ended up with my class ring at the end of the night. Years ago, boys would give their senior class ring to their girlfriend to wear around their neck or, like Mema, put enough tape on it to make it fit one of her fingers. After that night, we started seeing each other at school more often and started attending a music appreciation session together at noon. I had asked her for my ring back when I saw her at school, but she conned me into letting her keep it for a while. Mema was a convincing young lady when she wanted to be. Read more about this in the "How I Met Your Grandmother" story.

WHAT DID YOU DO ON YOUR FIRST DATE?

I do not remember each exact detail of our first date; however, I know we went to a drive-in movie and probably did a lot of soul-searching on our first date. A drive-in movie is a thing of the past; however, many years ago, we could drive our automobiles into this large field that had rows of outside speakers. We would hang the speakers on the window glass and hear the movie while we watched it from our automobiles. It was a fun situation especially if you liked your girl-friend to be close to you so you could whisper sweet nothings' in her ear, smell her perfume, and steal a kiss every now and then.

On a first date, one has to try to find some common ground on which to build a solid relationship. Then you find out her likes and dislikes and compare them to yours. I always wanted to please my girlfriends by acting in a way that they would not be skeptical or afraid of being alone with me. I wanted to gain their confidence so we could have a good time and have fun together. Mema was a very conservative young girl and would never let her guard down in any situation. She was basically in control then as she is now and has always been. She was a very respectful girl and well-liked by many of her peers as she was involved in many organizations during her grammar school and high school years. In fact, Mema was chosen as Ms. Colquitt County in a beauty queen contest two years con-secutively in 1949 and 1950, and then her popularity grew even greater after that. She also raised a steer for competition in the cattle show in Colquitt County, and her steer also won first place two years consecutively. Mema was a very special girl, and I knew it from the beginning of our relationship. It was known that Papa did not have much money to spend on a date, but that did not matter to Mema. There was a special drive-in restaurant on the way home from the movie, and on several occasions, I would ask Mema as we were pass-ing this place, the "Pig & Chick," if she wanted to stop for a drink. She would always say, "No, not tonight," and we would go on to her house. I asked her later why she always said no and she told me that "I always thought that you didn't have the money to spend, so I didn't want to stop." That was a very special girl and a very sensitive one as well to be so young.

HOW DID YOU PROPOSE?

Mema and I had dated for a long time, and we were in love with each other very much. I was in the Navy stationed in San Diego,

California, at Miramar Naval Air Station, a master jet base. I was selected to go on a detachment to South America: Coco Solo, Canal Zone. While there, I would write Mema every day and tell her about my accomplishments during the day and how much I loved her. One day, I got up enough nerve to write her a proposal letter, and I asked her to marry me when I returned back to the United States and returned home on leave. Now remember, we did not have access to telephones or quick communications, so I had to wait for about two weeks before I received her reply to my proposal. I received the letter, and she had accepted my proposal. We were engaged by mail. All my buddies thought I was crazy marrying a young girl and only making about $92 per month.

WHEN AND WHERE DID YOU GET MARRIED? WHAT DID YOU LIKE MOST ABOUT YOUR WEDDING?

While I was still in South America, Mema was planning our wedding and had already set the date. All I had to do was wait for her and her family to do all the planning and all the legwork. The night prior to our wedding day, Mema and I had a date. When I brought her home, I did not want to leave since I knew that I could not see her until the next night of our wedding. They say it is unlucky to see your bride the day of the wedding until she is brought down the aisle to meet you at the altar. It just seemed that I wanted to hang on to her a little longer that night; however, her father had rules that established a time for her to be home each evening from a date. This rule had to be strictly enforced.

On April 25, 1953, we were married in the dining room of her home. It was decorated very beautifully, and the home was packed with many of our family and friends. Prior to me remodeling the current home, the dining room was much smaller than it is now.

I liked my beautiful bride, Mema, most of all; and she was the center of attraction that night as well as the rest of my life. In my opinion, Mema was the highlight of the total celebration and my entire life. You cannot imagine what a sweet and wonderful lady Mema was back then and as she is today. She had me charmed from the get-go and took control of my life and did a good job of guiding me in the right direction.

This is a short story about my wedding night. It was raining very hard the night of our wedding, and back then all the roads in our area were not paved. Therefore, the dirt roads were very slick and dangerous to drive on unless you had a four-wheel-drive automobile. My stepmother's family had planned to come to our wedding but only knew one way to Mema's home, and that was coming by Sardis Church. At that time, the area just west of Sardis Church was steep, all clay dirt and very slippery and known as Sardis' Hill. It was almost impossible to drive down that hill in an ordinary automobile, so they missed our wedding because of the rain and a slippery hill.

WHAT HAVE YOU LOVED MOST ABOUT YOUR SHARED LIFE?

There are many things that I have loved and enjoyed about our shared life together. I guess that I married one of the most old-fashioned girls in the country to be so young. Mema was barely eighteen years old when we were married; however, she was much more mature for her age than many older women. She believes women should treat their men with respect and dignity but also rule with a firm hand. Mema has always been so compassionate and caring, more so than me. I have never had any reason during our married life to distrust her in any way. She has always been so faithful and loving to me in many ways and much more than I have ever deserved. God has truly blessed me with a wonderful, loving, and caring soul mate to share my life with. I would not swap her for anyone on the face of this earth and have never regretted marrying her and caring for her the best I could. She has always been a loving, caring, and God-fearing mother, grandmother, and great-grandmother to each of her offspring.

Each of you are blessed to have her as an example to live by and should be extremely thankful. We have been blessed to have each other to lean on for support whenever we had no other family member near us to comfort or console us; however, we consoled each other and put our trust in the Lord for guidance. Mema and I were two very young adults who were alone in a vast world extremely different from our home environment; however, we made the best of it and survived to tell you about it.

Mema's family was always very good to me and accepted me as one of their own from the very beginning of our life together. I did not associate with my father and stepmother for many years after Mema and I were discharged from the Navy. They were very difficult to talk to and less to understand that we had our own life to live. Grandpa and Grandma Norman adopted me as one of their own and treated me very well as long as they lived. They were exceptionally good folks.

SHARE WITH ME SOME SPECIAL MEMORIES YOU HAVE ABOUT YOUR LIFE WITH GRANDMA

When you have been married as long as Mema and I have (since April 25, 1953), there are many memorable memories to remember. Mema and I have had so many good times together that it is difficult to narrow it down to a few spaces on paper. After I returned from overseas and Mema came to Escondido, California, to live with me, we had a good time together reacquainting ourselves with each other. You see, we did not have a honeymoon as it is accustomed to do. We did not have any family out there, so we could not rely on anyone for assistance; nor did we have anyone but ourselves in the time of need or consolation. It was just us in a large town that we did not know much about. We sure had fun just being together and being by ourselves. At the end of my work shift, I could hardly wait to get to our apartment to be with her.

Of course, my first special memory was us getting married and starting to live together as husband and wife. Now that takes some getting used to in a hurry. One goes from being with their family and being taught not to do certain things to living with a total stranger whom one actually knows very little about. That is a good memory of how Mema and I got started.

Other great memories are when you know you are going to have a child together and then when they are actually born. During the rearing of your children, you have many special memories as well. Then when they get married, it is another good memory. The product of your children getting married is that they present you with grandchildren that are so special also. Then all the special memories come one at a time with your grandchildren until they get married as well. Once they get married and present you with great-grandchildren, which, by the way, are the BEST memories of all births. Our great-grandchildren are the highlight of Mema's and my life, and we have so many vivid special memories of you. Mema and I have shared most of them together with each of you children and have enjoyed you so much with the little things that you do to make us smile and to make us happy, which, by the way, did not take much.

Now that we are older and must spend a lot of our time by ourselves, we have lots of time to talk about our boys and the things they did and the things they said; and all this makes us happy. Each of you have a unique place in our hearts as all of you are so different in many ways and in some ways you are very similar.

As Mema and I met, dated, and fell in love, neither of us feel it was nothing but the Lord that brought us together and allowed us to remain together for so long. When you boys start dating, you will realize what we realized in our younger years. I had this special feeling for Mema that I had never had for any other girl that I dated. When I got enough nerve to hold her hand for long lengths of time, I could feel a little twitter in my body, and it just felt right. After we had dated for a length of time and she allowed me to kiss her good night at the end of our date, that sent special shivers down my spine, and I knew that Mema was the special one for me. No other girl had ever affected me the way Mema did. I felt in my heart that the Lord had led me to the mother of my children, and he blessed me with a great one. I was always told to treat my date as I wanted my sister to be treated, and that is good advice. My feeling for Mema has always been respectful and loving. Below is a letter I wrote to Mema on April 25, 1972, which happens to be our anniversary. We had been married for nineteen years, and I read this to her in our Sardis Church conference at our monthly meeting. The second is an article I wrote about my feelings for her on January 25, 2014, after we had attended a wedding at your great-grandmother's church, the Tabernacle on Cannon Road.

April 25, 1972
Dearest Virginia:

May I express my sincere appreciation and thanks for your tolerance and patience during the last nineteen years. You know, I can't realize that it has been nineteen years since I took you as my helpmate. The experiences have been so sweet; your help, beneficial; your devotion as a wife and mother, unquestionable; and your trust and confidence in my ability to perform my duties or go to school has been outstanding.

During our years together, I can think of a few things I would change for myself, if I could; but none for you. Your faith in God and me has never been questioned nor has your loyalty to me been doubted. Some of our years have been lean; but by the help of God, we have made them okay. As time passed, it seemed that we would not accomplish much; nevertheless, we have done very well for ourselves and our children.

As the years passed, I watched you grow from a sweet, little, inexperienced farm girl into a wonderful, experienced woman. I also observed your changes from a freckled-face, auburn-haired young girl into a beautiful gray-streaked middle-aged lady.

All in all, I have enjoyed being with you very much; and of all the millions of women in the world, I can't think of one that I had rather spend my remaining time with than you.

I hope God will continue to bless our union in the future and will give us reasonable health and much happiness to enjoy our children—and maybe our grandchildren too.

If any one element, other than God himself, deserves any credit for me being what I am (whatever that is), it is you. You have always stood behind me (nagging) with much encouragement and patience.

In closing, I would like to say that I love you very much and feel the way Ruth did when she wrote Ruth 1:16, 17. I hope God will spare me the sting of losing you by taking me first.

Signed,
Bud

OUR HOLY VOWS

by Homer (Papa) Eldridge
January 25, 2014

The other day, my wife, Virginia, and I attended a church wedding. It was a beautiful ceremony. I fought back tears. (I know men don't cry at weddings, do they?) Taking a swift glance at the lady seated to my left, I thought about our wedding, April 25, 1953. We made those same vows, and we were pronounced husband and wife. As I joined myself to Virginia that day through a very unique and special ceremony, my life totally changed, and so did hers. I pledged myself to her and her to me.

Sitting there in the church, I sort of lost myself in memories of how those vows have been tested through the many years, a total of sixty at this time. I saw my lovely bride out of the corner of my eye. Virginia has been so faithful to me and to the vows she pronounced in her home. And I have been faithful to her as well.

We have struggled; however, I am responsible for much of the strain put on our sacred pledges. Two becoming one is much easier said than done. Virginia has seen me at my worst, but our marriage has been preserved, severely tested, and found solid. The Author of that ceremony has kept us both safe from all kinds of evil and heartache.

Our marriage is secure not because of our efforts but because God heard our hearts speaking when we pronounced our vows. He engendered the powerful, supernatural endurance to produce the union we wanted; however, by ourselves, we were too weak to obtain.

Every wedding service of God's children is attended by the Master. He is present, front and center. He is witness to the vows we pronounce. To Him, they are more than words from a script. He watches us exchange the rings. He smiles as the groom, openly and unashamedly, kisses the bride. He laughs as the confetti is thrown and we rush to our car covered with "Just Married" slogans and streamers.

And we did not leave Him at the bride's home with the other well-wishers. At that time, I realized that I was now the head of a household and must assume the total responsibility for our family and its well-being. He becomes the Counselor, the Provider, and the "Holy Cement" that melds our union, seeing us through unemployment, spats, the birth of our children, and all the challenges of providing for a family. He consoles, comforts, and advises young wives and guides their clueless young husbands. He gives patience to both husband and wife and strengthens the union through each new crisis.

My thoughts concerning the ceremony end with wonder and amazement that Jesus can see this planted seed through to its full fruition.

Turning to get a full view of my bride's face, I am filled with thanksgiving for His faithfulness through the years. We have made many wonderful memories together, memories created by the Lover of our souls. I ask myself, how do couples ever make it without Him?

YOUR YOUNG FAMILY

———•———

WHAT DID YOU DO FOR A LIVING
WHEN YOU STARTED YOUR FAMILY?

When Mema and I married, I made a living being a sailor. I was in the Navy making $92 per month. When we married, my salary increased to $120.10 per month. We paid rent, a car payment, gas, food, and all our incidental bills from our meager salary. When I brought Mema and Larry to California, I started working part-time at Sears in San Diego; and I made as much there part-time as I did full-time in the Navy. This job really increased our spending capability greatly. I remained in the Navy until September 30, 1955, and remained with Sears until October 15, 1955.

After being discharged from the Navy, Mema and I came home to Moultrie to start our life in a new capacity. I looked all over for a job locally but could not find one here. We settled in Smyrna, Georgia, where I worked for an aircraft company called Lockheed. I worked there for about ten months before being hired at Moody AF Base as a jet engine mechanic. Mema was pregnant with Lynn, and we wanted to be near our family in Moultrie; therefore, we could have a better life together with all our family.

DID GRANDMA WORK? WHAT DID SHE DO?

Yes, Grandma did work while we were in Escondido, California, and before she became pregnant with Larry. She worked at a small store that they called a dime store back in those days. It was a place where they sold a lot of little inexpensive items and not much of it cost over a dollar. She did not work there very long because we moved to live on the Naval base at Miramar. She did not make much money, but it gave her a little extra to spend on herself. Mema did not work again until Lynn was about seven years old; and by that time we lived in Jacksonville, Florida. She waited until both Larry and Lynn were in school, and then she wanted to go to work so I could quit my second job and go to college. Mema worked at a small egg company on Edgewood Court for a short time. She was hired at Winn-Dixie, which was just a short distance from her starting job at Dixie Egg. Mema worked at Winn-Dixie for almost twenty-three years and then retired due to health problems in 1987.

Now remember that raising a family and taking care of their needs is an awesome job also. Mema worked hard at doing things for all of us and made sure that everyone was taken care of very well. Papa was away in the Navy on occasions, and Mema had to attend to all the business and take care of our children as well. This was a task within itself, and she managed the household as well.

WHERE WAS YOUR HOME, AND WHAT WAS IT LIKE?

We had several homes while we were stationed in California. Our first home was an upstairs apartment in Escondido, California, near our friends Jim and Earlyne Swanson. They assisted me in selecting the apartment before Mema came to live with me in California. It was a very small apartment; however, it was a nice cozy one just for the two of us. Mema did not like the apartment because she did not assist in selecting it, so we moved to another apartment downstairs in the same building. Not long after that, another apartment became available on the same property, and we moved into it. This was a much larger and nicer apartment than the others, and we enjoyed it. Mema became pregnant and was real sick from the smell of gas that we used in our cooking stove. We decided to move nearer to my base, so we rented a small mobile home on the base. This mobile home was nothing but a camping trailer as it was only eight feet wide and twenty-seven feet long and crowded to say the least. I was scheduled to go overseas again, so I brought Mema back to Georgia so she could be with her family while I was overseas and so she could give birth to Larry in Georgia.

We have actually had so many homes that it would be boring to tell you about all of them; however, Mema and I were always happy to be together in our home no matter what size it was or how it was built. I built us three homes in Clay County, Florida, and we loved all of them; however, the best one was in a subdivision called Foxwood on Kingsley Avenue. We lived there a little over twenty-three years, and that is when we met Mr. Jack and Ms. Kitty Keys, our good friend who now lives in Penny Farms. She and Mr. Jack brought us cold lemonade and refreshments when we were clearing our lot to build. After that we had many good times together. We left Foxwood and moved back to Georgia in April 1997 after Great-Great-Grandmother Ola Norman passed away on January 6, 1997. Great-Great-Grandpa Wheeler (JW) Norman had passed away in March 6, 1987. Mema inherited the old home and farm where some of her siblings were born and where all of them were raised. Uncle Lincoln is the oldest, and he has lived there since April 2, 1933. We started taking care of Uncle Lincoln when we moved to Georgia

WHAT MADE MY MOM LAUGH WHEN THEY WERE MY AGE?

It did not take much to make either of our granddaughters, Diana and Lisa, laugh when they were little. They were very happy little girls and would laugh at most of the things I would tell them. They always enjoyed my stories and our visits together. We were together a lot when they were little as Marsha was my material expediter when I was building homes in Duval, Baker, and Clay Counties. Diana and her parents (Larry and Marsha) lived with us for a year when they first moved to Orange Park from Georgia, and they both lived with us about a year when Gramps and Grammy sold their home on Morgan Circle Drive. We had good times together and ate often at the Famous Amos Restaurant on Blanding Boulevard. I would take them with me to inspect construction jobs and would also tell them stories as we went to and from the sites. I would also take them to the trash dump, and this would always seem to bring out some strange little things in each of them. Diana would like to go to Mr. Katabah's place as he would hold her while I did some chores for him because he was sick with cancer and not able to do much work. The girls would laugh a lot when we went to Disney World and do all the rides that they wanted and do other activities as well. They would also laugh a lot when we went to Georgia to visit Grandpa and Grandma Norman on the farm where there were always plenty of things to do and good things to eat. They were two very great people and would have loved all my boys the way they loved your mothers and the rest of the family. Not only did Diana laugh at many things but she also had all of us and our friends laughing at her. She would put on a show for anyone available to watch. We had a split-level den and kitchen in Foxwood, and the opening from the kitchen to the den was a perfect place for her to put on a show for us. While our friends were seated in the den, Diana would always come around and "take orders" from everyone for drinks and dessert. She was our model waitress but yet so young. Lisa was always too conservative to do something like this. One thing Lisa did to make us laugh was prepare lunch for Diana, who did not know how to prepare a sandwich or anything. Lisa would make her and Diana a banana-and-potato-chip sandwich for lunch. This made all of us laugh.

When your mothers, Diana and Lisa, were growing up and they did something for me, I would tell them, "I'll dance at your wedding," just as sort of a payback for them helping me with some projects. Later on when each of them were married, both told me as a gesture of love, "Don't you remember what you told us since we were little girls? You promised to dance at our wedding, so the time has come to fulfill that promise." I danced with each of them and that was the best dance of the night and we were the highlight of the night as each of them shuffled me around the dance floor. It was a promise kept, and I enjoyed every minute of it. The gist of this short story is a simple fact: if you make a commitment to someone, please keep it to the best of your ability!

HOW DID YOU SPEND TIME TOGETHER AS A FAMILY?

When we were in the Navy, we would spend our weekends with friends in California and ride in the mountains and explore the sights of the area. We would take Larry to the restaurants, and people would marvel at how chubby he was and also how cute he was. He would always attract attention in most areas that we traveled. He was a favorite to our good friends the Swansons and Shirley and Rich in Escondido.

Then we moved back to Georgia, and we spent a lot of time with Mema's folks and did a lot of things on the farm as you boys do as when you were growing up. Aunt Lynn was born on August 27, 1956, and we spent a lot of time trying to convince Larry that this was a good thing; however, he did not always see it that way.

We spent time going to the Boy Scouts for Larry and Brownies for Lynn. They were involved in taking music lessons, and we would spend time making sure that they practiced and had all their lessons prepared. I was a scout master for Larry's troop in Jacksonville, and one of my best friends was the camping and trip coordinator. We sent the boys to Tennessee one year, and they had a marvelous time on all the Civil War trails and received many merit badges for doing so. On the way back from Tennessee, they stopped at Grandpa Norman's farm and camped out in the cow pasture down near our current catfish hole.

We spent time going to different churches in Georgia and Florida after we moved there. Most Sundays we would go to McDonald's and eat lunch there and just have a good time together.

I worked a lot during the early years of both Larry and Lynn, so we did not have much time to spend going different places as there were not many places during their young years. We had no amusement parks, no Wild Waters, and no Disney World nor any of those fun parks that you have today.

We went to see Mema's parents in Moultrie very often and always had a fun weekend there. They had horses to ride and tractors to drive and many fun things to do. Larry learned to shoot a gun at a young age and went hunting with his uncles and his grandpa Norman. Lynn was always interested in cooking, and she helped Mema and her grandma Norman in the kitchen. That is one reason that she is such a great cook now.

WHAT ARE YOUR FONDEST MEMORIES OF RAISING A YOUNG FAMILY?

As I have stated prior to this, at my age, I have many wonderful fond memories of my life with Mema, Larry, and Lynn both as children and also as young adults and even now in their older years. The Lord has blessed me many times to be able to afford the things I awarded to our children. He has given us many years to enjoy them and their children and on to my great-grandchildren. I thought being a grandfather was a special event, and I always let my boys know that from the beginning. They were very special to Mema and me, and we would always express our love to them in verbal and physical expressions. Us giving them things that we could made us proud and thankful that the Lord had provided this for us. Remember, it is only loaned to us through our Lord because it all belonged to him in the beginning; he just gives it to us to share with others.

I guess the most gratifying thing to us is that we raised a couple of strong, independent, self-reliant, great-thinking, and trustworthy individuals, Larry and Aunt Lynn. During the time of their early childhood, we would make sure that they knew the right thing to do and the wrong thing NOT to do. We chastised our children from the early age, and they knew that we loved them; however, we wanted others to love and respect them as well. They may have thought it was tough at the time, but they knew how we stood on many issues. I believe that it paid us back many times during their developing and growing years. The Lord blessed us with two great children, and we could not have asked for more.

Both of them have been in many clubs and associated with many groups in their lifetime, and in most instances, they have been leaders and doers, not just a couple of standby people. Now that is a fond memory for both Mema and me, and now we can sit back in our older years and reflect on our accomplishments through our dependence on the Lord directing us. It has made both of us so proud to have Larry and Lynn as members of Sardis Primitive Baptist Church, and we are especially proud and honored the church believed Larry would be a good deacon and ordained him on November 26, 2004, to serve as one. I know when I leave this earth that the church will be in good hands.

BEING A GRANDPA

——•——

GRANDPA, DO YOU REMEMBER WHEN I WAS BORN?

Yes, I remember when each of you were born, and Mema and I were there for each of your births. There is a special joy in being at the birth of your great-grandchild. Grandchildren are special; however, great-grandchildren put the icing on the cake, so to speak. We also had great support from our friends and family in Orange Park. Ms. Kitty, Uncle Pat, and Aunt Clarice were also there to greet the new one into this world and their family. We stayed in the room with your mothers until it was time for each of your grand entrance, and then we had to leave for a short time so the doctor could do his thing. It was such a great feeling to see and hold you for the first time as Mema and I were back in the line as to who was to hold "our baby" for the first time. Surely, I let Mema hold you before I did because I wanted to save the best until last.

I did get to be with all of you and just thanked God that each of you were so pretty and healthy; we were blessed with that gift for each of you. You were no sweeter to me then than you are now; however, it is difficult for me to hold you as close to me as it was then. No reflection on any of my boys; however, I guess that being there when Punkin was born was one of the highlights of our life, our very own first great-grandson. We had waited nine months for his arrival, and it was fantastic; he broke the icing, so to speak.

It was a very special occasion when each of you were born, and it made our lives more complete with the addition of each of you.

The most memorable time was when Cameron was born and shown to all of us for the first time. Throughout Lisa's pregnancy, all of us saw the sonograms of our expected great-grandchild. Remember, each of these sonograms are in a dark contrast, and it made the baby (Cameron) look darker than he really was. Christopher was standing in front of me when he first saw his little brother in living form. Cameron was a little red but a lot of white. Christopher (Punkin) looked up at me and exclaimed, "Papa, he is white." All these months he had an image of his little brother being black; however, he never said anything about it to anyone in the family. There is no telling what goes through the minds of a little child. We were also there when Bradley and Blake were born and witnessed a very proud daddy (Uncle Stephen) showing off his boys from within the delivery room dressed in a sterile gown.

There are some circumstances in life that are not as pleasant as others. However, we must persevere and go on with our life the best possible. One case being that Christopher and Cameron's dad was not the type of dad he should have been in caring for and teaching his children the things that should be taught to a small child. After several circumstances, your mother made a choice to separate from him and raise you on her own with the help of the Lord and her family. After several years of uncertainty about what role your dad would play in your life, both of you boys decided to change your birth name from Thomas to Eldridge. This took a long time and lots of court time, but in the end, it all paid off. On September 22, 2014, the court ordered your surname to be changed from Thomas to Eldridge, and I do believe the world celebrated with each of you as this was accomplished. We were very proud that each of you had requested that this be done. Since that day, we have all rejoiced with each of you on the courts and your decision. May the Lord bless and keep each of you in his grasp and protect you from the likes of your dad.

WHAT WERE YOU DOING WHEN
YOU HEARD THE NEWS?

I was in the hospital waiting room waiting with anticipation with our friends and family, just waiting for the information that you were born and that everything was just fine with the baby and its mother. It was always such a relief to hear the doctor say the words we all were waiting for, "It's a boy, and he and the mother are doing great." Those were such comforting words to all of us, and then we all said a silent prayer to God thanking Him for you and making sure that He knew that we thought of you as a blessing from Heaven and that everything would be okay.

HOW IS BEING A GREAT-
GRANDPARENT FUN FOR YOU?

The English language does not have the superlatives or adjectives to describe how I feel about my boys at any given time. I always loved being around you and doing things with you and for you. It makes me very proud to have each of you help me with a project that you may have thought about or invented by yourself. All of you boys were so inventive and able to come up with some good projects for us to work on together. It also made it so good for us to spend time with each other.

Mema and I always look forward to coming to Fleming Island to see you boys and also looked much more forward to see you come to see us in Georgia. We loved to see you so much that we built a special little house for you to stay in so you could have your own space and privacy. That is the reason that we call it the boys' house; it is yours to stay in and enjoy. We always want each of you to feel like you can come to see us anytime you desire and feel more than welcome to stay either with us in the big house or in your house. And later when you have family, you can bring them to see us as well, and then we can spoil our great-great-grandchildren like we did you and your parents. Last but not least, it is so good being a great-grandparent when we can send you noisy little boys to your house and let us have a great peace and quiet in the big house.

WHAT DO YOU LIKE TO DO WITH YOUR GREAT-GRANDCHILDREN?

I like to do many things with my boys and look forward to doing it with them. I like to take you fishing or just going to the pond to look around at various things in the area. I love to take you riding on the big tractor and let you take turns driving since there are no police on the farm to stop our adventures. We love to have pizza parties at our house while you are visiting. We really love to have you go to Sardis Church with us and help sing the old songs from our noteless books. We did always love to go to theme and fun parks with you while we were younger; however, we are not as quick as we once were. Consequently, we do not have the strength to keep up with you boys and do the things that you want us to.

Just look at what happens to an old man when he races one of his boys (Punkin) on a bicycle or even when he plays soccer (Bradley and Cameron) with them. He falls and hurts himself and ends up in the doctor's office taking treatments and pain pills for being so foolish and careless. However, Papa always loves to get involved with you and your sports. We always loved to watch each of you competing in your sport, and we always enjoyed your game, competitiveness, and determination to win. I love to interact with all of you boys in the sports that you like. I also like to assist you in making various things in Aunt Lynn's garage with the screw guns and air guns. Each of you can do a great job with the guns, and sometimes you need no assistance at all. Papa tried to teach each of you how to safely use the tools of the trade. We have made boats, bird feeders, and birdhouses as well as other minor things with wood that you helped cut out for the project and screw together with my cordless gun.

WHAT DO YOU WANT YOUR GREAT-GRANDKIDS TO KNOW ABOUT YOU?

Obviously, Papa does not want you to know of the many things that I did wrong while growing up in a large family. I believe that I have written enough previously for you to sort of understand some of the things that I think are important for you to know, and maybe someone will fill you in on some of the things that I did not write about.

I want you to know my love for my God, my family, my country, my friends and relatives, and my fellow beings that surround me daily. Many of them have done so much for me, and "thanks" is just not enough in some circumstances; however, it suffices in most events or occasions. My God has looked after me all the days of my life, and many times I was not even aware of Him doing so, just like you are not aware of His presence either.

I also want you to know that each time I told you that I would do something for each of you, I really meant it in a loving way. Now it did not always work out the way we wanted it to; however, something good always happens to those that wait with patience. I would never directly lie to either of you on purpose, and I would be concerned if I knew that you would tell Papa a lie just to get around an issue. It is not worth it to either of us, and it indicates mistrust between each of us when we do things such as that. Let's always be honest with one another; however, I know from experience that it can make things a little testy at times, but we can work through the issues if we love and understand one another.

I guess I want my legacy to say to those that I have left here on earth is that "my Papa loved living and always enjoyed his family very much. He enjoyed seeing them happy and also enjoyed giving, especially when they least expected the gift or treat."

HOPE AND A FUTURE

———•———•———

GRANDPA, DO YOU REMEMBER
WHAT YOU DREAMED ABOUT
ACCOMPLISHING? HAVE YOU DONE IT?

When I was just a kid growing up in Orlando, Florida, I cannot remember dreaming of doing much of anything other than playing with my friends and relatives in our neighborhood. I had never been out of the state of Florida except for an occasional trip to Moultrie, Georgia, nor any other place than in the vicinity of Orlando and its surrounding communities.

I did go to the movies and watch all these things happen to the actors; however, I knew that was played as our entertainment and not for real-life examples.

In a few years we moved to Colquitt County, Georgia, and things changed drastically. After working in the tobacco and cotton fields doing manual labor, I dreamed that I wanted to get out of that cotton patch and do something productive with my life. I did not know exactly what I was going to do, but I knew it would be better than the tobacco or cotton patch and a lot better financial benefit to me.

Yes, the Lord has allowed me to accomplish much more than I ever expected to accomplish when I left high school in 1951.

As I review my life from the time I joined the Navy until the present, I can see that the Lord was in control all the time, and I just did not realize it. He has guided me through many tough and disappointing times only for me to realize later that he had bigger and better things for me to do. I always wanted a different position at the base but failed to get it. Later the Lord led me to a better job with much better pay and more responsibility than the previous job I applied for. It happened more than one time, so I know that it was not just a coincidence in life. I had help from a Higher Power.

So the answer to your question is YES. I always wanted to be respected by my family, friends, and loved ones; and I believe that from all indications demonstrated to me, I am. Another dream of mine was to be loved by my grandchildren and by my great-grand-children as I loved my grandfather, Homer Eldridge. And from all indications received by my brain, I have finally accomplished that goal as well. It is so great to be the center of attention with my boys in a crowd, just as if nobody else was there. It thrills my heart to see those little faces looking up to me, eagerly wanting me to see what they have done or for them to tell me something that they have done recently. It just doesn't get any better than that, and the Lord has blessed me again and again with circumstances and events. With all four of them with me and each of them wanting my attention to tell me something or show me something, what better peace could a man have than that?

Therefore, I want each of you to always have a dream of aspiration for achieving bigger and greater things in your life. Here is a poem written by Amanda Bradley that says it better than I can. Success comes from hard work, patience, and the help of the Lord.

ALWAYS HAVE A DREAM

Forget about the days when it's been cloudy,
But don't forget your hours in the SUN...
Forget about the times you've been defeated,
But don't forget the VICTORIES you've won...

Forget about mistakes,
That you can't change now,
But don't forget,
The lessons that you've learned...

Forget about misfortunes
You've encountered,
But don't forget
The times your LUCK has turned…

Forget about the days
When you've been lonely,
But don't forget
The friendly SMILES you've seen…

Forget about the plans
That didn't seem to work out right,
But don't forget to
ALWAYS HAVE A DREAM.

WHAT HAVE YOU ENJOYED MOST ABOUT YOUR WORK?

I started working for hire when I was about ten years old for my grandfather who was a cook a local restaurant. I washed dishes for a dollar a night and worked about nine to ten hours. I did not mind the job or the hours because it provided me with some spending money and allowed me to save some as well.

Later on, after working on the farm for several years, I joined the Navy and learned an aircraft mechanic trade that would help me for many years both in the Navy and as a civilian government employee. I always enjoyed working on aircraft engines, and it made me feel good to know that my work helped provide the United States with an aircraft that could do its functions very well and also be safe for our aviators. I worked for seventeen years as a mechanic in one expertise or another. I had done well in my mechanical career and was promoted to an office position in January 1966. From that month until I retired from government civil service on May 1, 1987, I held several high-level positions and worked in Washington, DC, and many other states to assist in the management of our aircraft and aircraft engine rework programs. It was always a pleasure for me to go to work in the morning as I enjoyed my work and enjoyed the people I worked with or the ones that worked for me. I always treated my employees as an adult, and we functioned very well together.

Papa seemed to always have a second job when he was supporting his young family, and I was also learning other trades as well. I worked in service stations, Sear's mechanical sections, transportation companies, and managed a new home construction company for Mema and me. Larry, Marsha, and Mema helped when they could, and we worked well as a team on specific phases of construction.

I have always enjoyed working and showing some progress as I did whatever I planned to do. It seems that I look for things to do when most of the people my age are trying to do as little as possible. Just remember, when you want a project done, give it to a busy person, and they can handle it very well.

ON YOUR BIRTHDAYS, WHEN YOU BLOW OUT CANDLES, WHAT WISH COMES TO MIND?

I can never remember actually having a birthday cake made for me when I was a kid. There were too many of us to do that, and it cost money for all the frills of a birthday party. I have never been a big fan of making a wish when I blow out candles. I am a firm believer in God, and I do not believe that making a wish for anything accomplishes your goals in life. Sorry, I know that you boys have always had fake birthdays and real birthdays and you blow out candles at all of them; however, you think back and see how many of your wishes have come true from your birthday wishes.

WHAT ARE YOUR WISHES FOR ME, GRANDPA? FOR ALL YOUR GRANDCHILDREN AND GREAT-GRANDCHILDREN?

My wishes are the same as my prayers to our God in Heaven. I pray that all my family will continue to grow in grace and knowledge of our Lord and practice the same. It is also my prayer that you continue to be in good and reasonable health as you grow into viable young women and men and go your separate ways and have a good family of your own. I would also like to enjoy your life and successes as long as I can and experience the birth of some of my great-great-grand-children. I do not believe that is asking the Lord too much, seeing that He has allowed many of our family to live long productive lives. I would like for you to know right from wrong, good from bad, and to understand the difference.

I truly want each of you to be honest and trustworthy to your-selves and to others, especially to your family that has supported you all these years through many adversities and hardships. Also, be respectful of others as you go through life and show them the cour-tesy that you want from them and others; things just go better when everyone respects one another and puts a little empathy in their feel-ings toward others.

In other words, be good little boys all your life, and others will want to associate with and be around you.

One thing I would like to challenge each of you with as you grow in love and grace is to watch out for one another and remember that you will disagree on many things in life and you may even have some serious arguments; however, I want to challenge each of you to not let pride or a misunderstanding come between any of you. You will also find out in life that, at times, your wives will try to come between each of you. Please have the forethought and integrity to separate fact from fiction and work all these problems out before splitting up your family.

WHAT ARE THREE THINGS YOU STILL WANT TO TRY, SEE, OR DO IN YOUR LIFETIME?

I seriously want to TRY to live long enough to SEE your children born as I did you and DO the things for them that I have done for each of you sweet young men. This would be one of the most rewarding things the Lord could allow me to do as I depart this earth and join him in our eternal home.

At my age, there are not a lot of things that I can look forward to doing at any great pace or enduring strength. However, I can sit on the sidelines and watch my boys in action, and hopefully, they will participate in their sports in a good Christian manner and show others just how to behave. You must also act like a gentleman in all situations, even the most strenuous ones.

One last thing that I would love to see is that all of us function in unity and stop all this fighting and killing over so many frivolous matters as they do. This world would be a better place if everyone would respect one another and reserve the right to be different but function as one body; otherwise, agree to disagree but function together for the cause of the country or company. Just think what would happen if a part of your body would not want to function as it should and wanted to be the premier organ or part. It would be devastating to the rest of your body and would put a stop to all functions. Read 1 Corinthians 12:12–27 and see what the Lord said about the same type of situation.

You asked me for three things, but I will give you the forth thing for free. Papa wants the Lord to allow him to work until He calls me home to be with Him. I have always enjoyed working and especially for my friends and family. It is a known fact that I take my tools with me wherever I go, even on vacation. It has always been a privilege and honor for me to accomplish something for my friends and family and also know that they appreciate my efforts. God gave me special talents, and I try to use them to the best of my ability. I want you to use yours wisely as well.

LIFE LESSONS

————•————

WHAT HAVE YOU LEARNED THAT YOU
WANT TO PASS ALONG TO ME?

This question could be answered in many ways, and it would take me a long time to write you an answer; however, I will attempt to make it simple and somewhat spiritual and common sense. Papa has learned many things that may help each of you if you abide by some simple rules and just utilize common rationale to find a solution.

I have learned that I cannot do everything I want to do for several reasons. One, I could not afford the project, and I had to understand that before starting it. Another is I could not go through life alone as I needed someone of character to help me along the pathway of life. I chose Mema for that role, and she has been good for and to me through all our life together. So the lesson of this is, be careful when you choose a girlfriend, and make sure she has the same basic values that you do. Choose one that is God-fearing and loves the Lord as I hope you do. Make sure she does not have too much excess baggage (drugs, bad habits, wild side of life, drinking problem, etc.) when you get involved. Watch for various signs of irregular behavior and observe her immediate family as well for signs of instability and unusual behavior.

Be patient in life and consider others around you that you may never intentionally offend your relatives or friends. Be considerate of others, and do to them as you want to be treated. Be sure to think of the things you say to others as some bad things you say cannot be recalled; once said, it is over. Scripture verifies that in Matthew 25:14–30. Read this carefully and comprehend it well.

WHO GAVE YOU SOME OF THE BEST ADVICE EVER? WHAT WAS THAT ADVICE?

I received advice from many people in my life, and a lot of it sort of runs together when you try to think of an individual giving you the best advice ever. I received good advice from my grandfather, Homer Eldridge, when I worked for him in a couple of restaurants. Work hard and do your work good the first time so you will never have to do it over again. Some people say that if you have time to do it over, you must have had time to do it correct the first time. Makes sense, doesn't it?

My dad always told me many things to do and tried to give me an illustration when explaining how I should do and act. He as well told me that hard work normally pays off when you have a goal to strive for in life. Also, be true to yourself as you are the only one that really knows when you are truthful or not; you do not need a lie-detector test to know this as the Lord knows as well.

Use the talents the Lord gave you to the best of your ability; if not, He will remove them from you as quickly as He gave them to you. Let me give an undisputable example: read Matthew 25:14–30, and you will see what I am talking about. One can use this scripture in many ways.

Do not ever fret about someone doing better than you because we all do not and cannot have the same ability to function. Realize that you are better at some things than others and they are better at certain things than you are. In most cases, you will be rewarded for your efforts if not your accomplishments.

The two mentioned above are just two examples of people that inspired me to do the things that I have done to and for others. I have had many more during my working career that guided me through the paths of successful leadership and through my military career. One thing about it, you will know these people when you see them and how they talk to you. Good advisors will look at you while they give you instructions. They talk to you and not down to you or try to make you feel inferior.

WHICH TRIALS MADE YOU STRONGER?

I have had many trials in my life, and it seems that I learned a little from each one of them. Some trials are caused by the individual, and one cannot see the problem because we are too close to it. I have had trials in my work, in my family, in the military, in church, and even in our neighborhood. One must react to their trials differently in each group as some take a more-harsh reaction than others. Example, one would not have the same reaction to a family member that he would in the workplace or military. When we make mistakes, we sometimes cause our own trials to surface, and then we have to deal with them as nobody else can.

The Bible illustrates that all will have trials and tribulations in life; however, we must depend on the Lord to help us through them daily and pray that we do learn from our own mistakes. I want to share with you a poem written by Paula Finn. This poem illustrates the struggles of life and how to handle them:

You're on a journey where each experience will
teach you something valuable and you can't get
lost, for you already know the way by heart.
You're on a journey that is universal yet uniquely personal,
and profound yet astonishingly simple where sometimes
you will stumble and other times you will soar.
You'll learn that even at your darkest point, you
can find a light—if you look for it.
At the most difficult crossroad, you'll have
an answer if you listen for it.
Friends and family will accompany you part of the way, and you'll
walk the rest by yourself; however, you will never be alone.

Travel at your own pace. There'll be time enough to learn all you need to know and go as far as you're meant to go. Travel light. Letting go of extra baggage will keep your arms open and your heart free to fully embrace the gifts of the moment.

You may not always know exactly where you're headed, but if you follow the desires of your heart, the integrity of your conscience, and the wisdom of your soul, then each step you take will lead you to discover more of who you really are; and it will be a step in the right direction on the journey of a lifetime.

WHAT DO YOU WANT ME TO KNOW WHEN I AM CHOOSING A CAREER OR LIFE PATH?

I would like for you to investigate whatever occupation you want to pursue as a career. First, make sure that you enjoy the vocation and that the vocation will bring you happiness and prosperity. I mostly loved the jobs that I was doing, and I believe I did them well. I had very little college experience but grew up using good common sense and the old "hard work" ethic. Try to evaluate the position to see if there is potential for promotion and that you do not end up in a dead-end job with no potential of expanding or progressing. I know you boys often get bored when you do some repetitive chores with little or no action; therefore, you need to look ahead for many things to do that can promote your initiatives and ambitions in life. Be open-minded about swapping jobs if you desire more and better things like starting your own business or expanding the one that you have. Normally, a career chooses you, and you do not choose a career.

WHAT DO YOU HOPE THAT I WILL LEARN EARLY IN LIFE?

Papa hopes that each of you will learn to respect your parents and other elders as the Bible admonishes you to do. Nothing is more repulsive that to hear a kid that thinks he knows more than any adult in the group. Please learn to, as Blake told us, "Listen and learn."

Also, learn to organize your plans and execute your plans after thinking them through prayerfully. Be forthright with yourself and others and cultivate a sense of belonging to an organization or group. Be sociable and interact with others, and swap ideas that may assist you and your friends in working together as a team and not as an individual who boastfully knows everything and can do everything.

Another great trait in a successful, sweet young man is to be patient and considerate with the ones that have helped you through so many trials and difficulties. Like Cameron once told his mother, Aunt Lisa, "You gotta do what you gotta do." A very wise statement for a five-year-old.

INSPIRATION

PAPA, DID YOUR FATHER TEACH YOU A SPECIAL CRAFT?

Yes, he did. My dad was a great carpenter and trim finisher. He had worked at this trade since I was born in 1933 and continued to do so until his supervisor made him retire in 2000, just two years before he died at the age of eighty-five. As long as I can remember, I always wanted to please my dad in whatever I did. I watched him as he worked with wood of many kinds and many forms. He could plan, lay out, and execute plans for most any structure he set his mind to do so. He taught me how to use and care for all the tools of the trade; and believe me, tools, as everything else, have changed very much in the past thirty to forty years. He was about the best general "all around" carpenter that I ever knew. Even in his older years, I would call upon him to assist me in laying out certain projects while remodeling our home in Georgia. You see, I watched him to learn a trade and not to think that I knew more than he did in his trade. It helps to be patient and trust your instructor of any trade. Just like you boys using my screw gun and doing such a good job, you watched Papa and did as you should to do a good job building your ships, birdhouses, and bird feeders. Each of you learned very well and were fast learners as I was patient with each of you during our training period. I always enjoyed working with you boys, and it was good to see you learn something new.

DID YOU ENJOY PAINTING, DRAWING, READING, OR WRITING AS A BOY?

I sure did. I always looked toward the time that I could help my dad do the house building or house repairs. My dad taught me how to use a paintbrush and also how to care for one after each use. Paintbrushes will last a long time when you care for them the way you are supposed to, when you wash and clean them after each use.

I have always liked to draw. I was not as good as you boys; however, I did okay. I drew the plans for all the homes that I built for Mema, Gramps and Grammie, and Aunt Lynn. I did not do as good as a draftsman, but the home was built as designed and to state codes.

I did not have very much time to read when I was a kid as I had to work on the farm and do my homework as well. I have enjoyed reading some books and mostly the Bible. This is one of the most inspiring books one can read, and you learn every aspect of life if you watch for all the rules and guidelines provided.

WAS THERE A COLOR YOU LIKED MOST OF ALL?

I cannot ever remember having a favorite color; if I did, I cannot remember what it was. We colored a lot of books as a kid and just used the color that we thought fit the design of the picture or the situation (example, painting a girl, boy, animal, or a house or other object).

WHAT KIND OF MUSIC OR SCENERY INSPIRES YOU?

I guess that I love the songs from our old Lloyd hymnals at our Primitive Baptist churches, which have no musical notes in them, more than any other songs. However, my next most favorite music is religious or gospel songs and hymns. Mema and I listen to religious songs most every time we travel to and from Florida, Georgia, and on other trips. We favor the Statler Brothers albums more than any other; however, we do listen to some CDs about other things that our family has given us. Most all the songs we sing at church have a message that we could live by or die by.

I would also say the scenery in the mountains has to be one of the most impressive in the world and one of my favorite. One can just see how the Lord has made so much beauty in one area. I know that there are beautiful scenes in most all parts of the country and the world; however, none are as impressive as the mountains in the fall. Mema and I have driven through the mountains of Colorado and Arizona, and that view is very impressive as well. Also, think about the ocean; in many cases, it never overflows nor does it get out of its boundaries. It continues in the same pattern as always and hides many secrets within its depth.

WHAT DO YOU TREASURE MOST?

I will always treasure the thought that our Lord Jesus paid the ultimate sacrifice for all of His children, and it did not cost us a thing but gave us a lot. He had to love us to go through all He did for us, and what we need to do is revere His name above all others and serve no other gods other than Him.

I also treasure the love for my family most and especially the love that I have for and receive from Mema. Her love and support for me has never faltered even though sometimes she did not agree with me 100 percent; however, she stuck by me. I also treasure the trust that is shown to me by my family, friends, and coworkers throughout my career.

I also treasure being with my boys whenever I can very much, and I have learned so much about unconditional love from you. It seems that you always enjoy being around Papa as much as I enjoy being around you, if that is possible. Below is a poem that describes how I attempted to act and talk in a way that you would always be proud of me instead of not wanting to share your time and thoughts with me. I have always attempted to listen to your conversations and you telling me about your achievements with an open heart and an open mind. I want you to always look up to me no matter how tall you are in stature.

A LITTLE FELLOW FOLLOWS ME

A careful man I want to be
A little fellow follows me;
I do not dare go astray,
For fear he'll go the same way.
I cannot once escape his eyes;
What'er he sees me do, he tries;
Like me he says he's going to be
The little fellow who follows me.
He thinks that I am good and fine,
Believes in every word of mine;
The base in me he must not see,
The little fellow who follows me.
I must remember as I go
Through summer's sun and winter's snow,
I am building for the years that be
For the little chap who follows me.

TRADITIONS TO BUILD ON

—————•—————

PAPA, DO YOU REMEMBER WHEN YOU
AND YOUR PARENTS CELEBRATED
FAMILY TRADITIONS?

We celebrated all traditional holidays as well as other families did. We did not have anything of our family origin to celebrate as I remember. It was always traditional for us to go to church each Sunday and celebrate the Lord's day together. It was also traditional for us to grace our food prior to each meal and ask the Lord to bless the food that He had furnished and our family had prepared. We still carry out these traditions today as all my boys agree to bless our food before each meal no matter what it is and even if it had been blessed at a prior meal. One can never thank the Lord too much for all He has done for us or will do for us.

DID YOU START NEW TRADITIONS WHEN
YOUR CHILDREN WERE BORN?

I guess Mema and I did start a new tradition when our children were born. Since I cannot remember celebrating our birthdays as you and your family does (fake birthdays and real birthdays), we did celebrate our child's birthday each year with a traditional birthday cake with candles and all the trimmings. However, since Larry (Gramps) was born on August 28, 1954, and Aunt Lynn was born on August 27, 1956, we had a problem when to celebrate. I guess we learned very early that the children could remember when we celebrated their birthday better than we did, so we had to keep good records so we would not goof-up on the timing of their celebrations. I guess we did celebrate each of their birthdays individually at times, but it was not that often.

WHAT LEGACIES DID YOUR PARENTS OR GRANDPARENTS PASS TO YOU?

I guess legacy could be interpreted to be many things; however, I will guess you mean traits or mannerisms. Both my dad and grandfather instilled into me the rewards of working hard for the things you wish for. Both of them worked hard and worked most of their lives for much less than we have achieved in our life. Times were tough in my early years, and little things we wanted were few and far between. Hopefully, I can leave you a little of my desire to work and achieve more for your family. There has been a saying in my time that "there are no free lunches in life"; someone has to work and pay for them.

One other thing we were taught was not to expect the government to give us handouts. I can truthfully say that I nor any of my first-line siblings have never expected anything or received compensation from the government that we did not earn. That is a legacy that we are proud of in this day and time. All but one of my brothers served in the military; and Uncle Gene, Uncle Pat, and I retired from the military. Both of Aunt Betty's husbands, Uncle Jabe Sherertz and Uncle Jack Burke, retired from the Navy as well as my stepfather, Harold Ormston.

IS THERE A TRADITION YOU HOPE I WILL SHARE WITH MY CHILDREN SOMEDAY?

Yes. I hope that you and your children will earnestly worship our Lord as He should be worshipped. Please do not deem the time you spend in church or helping someone else as a chore or a waste of time. One is supposed to help others as he wants to be helped when needed.

Each of our family members have their own way of worshipping our Lord, and I consider that as a personal matter just as long as you do it earnestly and with dignity.

Teach them the things that you have been taught, and all will be well with you and your children. However, also remember the things that you resisted and do not be too hard on your children when they resist you as you did your parents. Be tolerant and patient. Proverbs 13:24 states, "He that spareth his rod hateth his son: but he that loveth him chasteneth him betimes." This can be interpreted as training him and not always punishing him.

HAPPY HOLIDAYS

———•———

HOW DID YOU CELEBRATE EASTER, THANKSGIVING, AND CHRISTMAS?

Our family always celebrated Thanksgiving and Christmas with a large meal and happy times of all of us being together. Easter was celebrated in a little different manner as it was mostly for small children and egg hunting.

However, each of the holidays are special as they represented a special legacy honoring our Lord in one way or another.

We knew that Jesus was born during the time set aside by someone as Christmas. It has changed from honoring Jesus to being very commercial and all about giving gifts instead of honoring the most precious gift of all, Jesus. Easter is dedicated to honoring the time that our Jesus rose from the dead after His crucifixion on the cross. It is a solemn time for a lot of people; however, it, too, has also become a commercial holiday. Our Jesus suffered too much to make this remembrance a festive occasion; it should be a time of solemn celebration showing our appreciation for His gift to us.

Thanksgiving is a man-made time to celebrate the early time when the Pilgrims thanked God for their bountiful harvest and they shared it with their neighbors, the Indians. We should always be thankful to our Lord for all His blessings to us and not just on special occasions.

I always love to be with my family during Christmas as we had such a wonderful time together. I joined the Navy in October of 1951 and was shipped to boot camp in San Diego, California.

Boot camp is fourteen weeks long with no interruptions whatsoever. Christmas was getting closer, and it appeared that we were not going to be able to go home due the restrictions of boot camp. I did not know if I could tolerate that or not and was very concerned about missing Christmas at home with the family. However, someone was looking out for us and gave the ones that wanted to go home permission to do so. That was a glorious time for a lot of us sailors. About sixty of us sailors climbed on a Greyhound bus in San Diego and rode it straight through to Berlin, Georgia, with sailors getting off on the way. That was a good Christmas as I surprised my family with my untimely arrival.

WHICH HOLIDAY IS YOUR FAVORITE?

I love all three of the holidays mentioned in the caption. However, due to the reason for the season, I like Christmas a little better than the others. One of the by-products of Christmas is the gift giving, which sometimes is very interesting and sometimes surprising. I have always loved to have a special gift for Mema, Larry, and Lynn throughout the years. Now it is the joy of watching my boys unwrap their gifts with the element of surprise and the comment "I have always wanted one of these" or "I have never had one of these before" and probably having a closet full of very similar toys. However, it was always fun to watch my boys have fun and know that they were blessed by God to have things such as that given to them. I always thought there were too many toys and not enough clothes. That is just your old conservative Papa talking.

WHAT DO YOU LIKE TO DO NOW DURING THE HOLIDAYS?

I love to spend my holidays with my family and friends. It is always good to share your time and food with family. When I was in the Navy, I would drive many miles to be home for our holiday celebration with my family. Papa has driven five hundred miles to be home for the holiday. It just meant so much to be with the ones you love. My family and Mema's family always loved to cook a lot of food and desserts for the holidays; therefore, we always had a lot left over for sandwiches and other stuff. I remember one year, we had sandwiches for a couple of days; and when we were preparing lunch at another time, Lisa asked, "Are we having that again?" She must have had enough turkey, huh?

WHAT WAS YOUR FIRST THANKSGIVING WITH GRANDMA LIKE?

It was great. I had just returned from overseas in September of 1953, and Mema had traveled to California to join me so we could be together, which was very special to me. As I have mentioned prior to this, our friends Jim and Earlene Swanson were always ready to share time with us as they fell in love with Mema from the very beginning and the feeling was mutual. Our first Thanksgiving was celebrated with them in Escondido, California, along with Earlene's parents, Mom and Dad Zickefoose, who owned a farm near our apartment. These people were just like our second family as they adopted Mema and me into their family and demonstrated no partiality between any of us.

DID YOU EVER RECEIVE OR GIVE A GIFT THAT WAS EXTRA SPECIAL?

Yes, I did. With the chance of sounding like a "Bible thumper," as I have been called, I received my greatest gift without even knowing it. Our Lord gave His only Son for our sins. That was a gift from our Savior Jesus Christ that we did not even earn or deserve. Now if this seems a little deep for you to understand, just ask Gramps, Uncle Stephen (Daddy), Aunt Lynn, your mommy, or Grammy.

My second-best gift was when we were married; Mema gave me my wonderful wedding band. As she did not have much money to spend, it was a simple wedding band; however, it is very sentimental to me. I loved it and would not trade it for anything as I still have it. However, in January 1966, I was promoted to an office job and was not in jeopardy of hanging my ring on engine or aircraft parts. On April 25, 1966, our anniversary, Mema gave me my current diamond wedding band. It is a beautiful three-diamond wedding band, and I have worn it with pride and love since that time. I have had many comments over the past years about how beautiful it is, and I tell them the story. I hope that my gift of a large diamond ring to replace the one I purchased before we were married was special to Mema. The first one I purchased was from a jewelry store in Escondido, California. Earlene helped me choose the right one that I could afford, and I purchased the wedding ring set on a payment plan that we could afford at that time. Once I paid it in full, the owner of the store gave Mema and me a toaster and coffee percolator, which came in good at that time since we were just beginning our life together.

Other things that Mema and I have given to Gramps, Grammy, Diana, and Lisa are gifts of love and necessity. We gave Gramps and Grammy cars and trucks so they would have a better and safer ride for them and our little girls. When they were old enough, we gave Diana a car when she was a senior at Orange Park High School; and she was the talk of her class because it was a Cadillac de Ville. Also, when Lisa was old enough, we gave her a Buick that we purchased from Aunt Rose McGee. It was a nice car, and she enjoyed it as well. When things are given in love, there are no strings attached; and our love for our family was unconditional—that means that they owed us nothing in return.

CHANGING TIMES

PAPA, DO YOU REMEMBER WHEN THERE WEREN'T COMPUTERS OR CELL PHONES?

Yes, I remember those days very well. We did not have a telephone when we lived in Orlando or in Georgia either. We still did not have a telephone in our home when I joined the Navy in October 1951. Grandpa Norman had a telephone in his home; however, he had three other families on the same circuit. Only one family at a time could use the telephone, which was a hassle most of the time. I was overseas in Alaska when Gramps was born, and Mema had to send me a telegram by Western Union to notify me of his birth.

Cell phones did not become very popular until the mid-1970s, and I had one installed in my truck at a cost of $950. Cell phones were very expensive when initiated for personal use. I still have my first handheld portable cell phone, and it is about the size of a large drill.

The new cell phones have almost unlimited capabilities and growing with each new model release. In October 2014, I purchased a smartphone, and I enjoy it very much. Some of these phones are replacing the computers as one can do any function on a cell phone that he can do on a computer. All my family members have all the functions needed and then some. I purchased my first computer in the 1980s, and we were very limited on its functions. The printer's paper had holes in the both sides, and the paper would scroll out when you initiated the print button. Due to my lack of training, I was very limited on the things I could do with it until Aunt Lynn would come home and show me more functions. I gradually learned more and more until I was able to do a lot of functions including e-mailing and making folders to store loads of information. I am now able to share e-mails and Facebook with family and friends on either my computer or cell phone. Isn't that great?

WHAT ARE THE BEST CHANGES THAT HAVE TAKEN PLACE DURING YOUR LIFETIME?

It has been said that there have been more innovations initiated in my generation than any other. It is amazing to see the advancement of technology within the last forty or fifty years in all facets of trades.

It would be difficult for me to isolate a single invention that stands out as the best change. Many improvements have occurred in all trades, and I have been involved in only a few (for example, construction and roofing have been my main endeavor). We have gone from installing our nails with hammers to using all types of pneumatic guns for all facets of my job in construction. Just an example, measuring tapes have been upgraded from a folding wooden tape to some sophisticated measuring devices including lasers.

Other great innovations have been made in the aircraft industry. Look at a 1945 airplane with the old reciprocating engines, and then compare it to one of our newest stealth aircraft powered by a sophisticated jet engine. Papa could provide you with many other examples, but I have only a limited space.

All appliances have been upgraded to many more functions and are much more convenient to operate. Medical practices have developed into a surprising modification of the body. When I was a child, there was no such thing as transferring body parts from one person to another nor repairing most internal body parts. In September of 2001, I had my heart taken from my body, had five blocked arteries repaired, and then had my heart placed back into my body. This action, along with the grace of God, prolonged my life so I could see my boys and enjoy them.

Medicines have made a great stride in helping to prolong life, also by God's grace.

WHAT DO YOU MISS ABOUT THE OLD DAYS?

There were many things that were good in the "old" days, but that is only in our memories. In the earlier days, we had most of our parents here to associate with, and many memories were made with them that cannot be erased. However, life is a revolving cycle, and that is the way God made it.

In the "old days," a person could give his word of agreement to a person with a handshake, and it meant something to each of them. It WAS a contract. Now, even with all the paperwork generated, a lot of agreements are trampled on as nothing that matters to anyone. In the old days, "a man's word was his bond." It's not so today.

However, if time did not progress, we would never have our children, grandchildren, and our precious great-grandchildren. So you see, it's better left the way it is. Our space program has been the initiative for many changes in many areas of manufacturing and food products that make it better for us. Progress must move forward.

IN WHAT WAY WAS YOUR CHILDHOOD A LOT DIFFERENT THAN MINE?

One thing for sure, I never had the things either of my boys has as a child. Also, there were more of us in my family than in either of your families, and we had to share more than you do. In my younger years, we moved several times and had to get adjusted to our new environment each time.

My younger years and up until I joined the Navy were more disciplined than yours, and I guess that was not all bad. However, I did know where my dad stood on many conditions and situations. I learned how to behave in church at an early age and knew the consequences if I did not.

My life was split in half when I was about six years old at the separation of my parents, and this was a devastating part of all our lives because we did not know exactly what happened to our parents. One day we were a happy functioning family, and the next day we did not have a mother to confide in or to be an intercessor between us and our dad when things came up. I hope and pray that this does not happen to either of you boys and your wives.

Technology is much greater now than in my younger years, so you have a better advantage of learning more and learning faster than me. Additionally, you are informed of all events of the world almost instantaneously via satellite and news devices.

You have had the opportunity to travel to many places that I never knew existed until I was older. You have many more amusement and theme parks than we had as we did not have any, and we lived in Orlando. We did have the opportunity to go swimming each evening in a lake near our home, and that part of the day was enjoyable.

HOW WAS IT SIMILAR?

I guess it was similar in some ways since each of our families go to church together and we did a lot of functions together as yours does. We played often with our friends, cousins, and siblings as you play with your cousins and your siblings.

It was also similar since we had a grandfather (on my father's side) and a grandmother (on my mother's side) to depend on and talk to when we needed help or someone to take up for us or care for us.

SHARING BETWEEN GENERATIONS

———•————•————•———

DO YOU HAVE SOMETHING SPECIAL THAT BELONGED TO YOUR MOTHER OR FATHER?

Yes, I do. When my father passed away, he left most of his belongings to his youngest son, Charlie Ray (my half brother—we had the same dad but different mothers), and his grandchildren by Charlie Ray. After all the things were divided and the estate settled, Charlie Ray brought my dad's old sixteen-gauge shotgun over and asked if I wanted this gun. My answer was definitely yes. I can remember when my dad kept that gun in a special place in our home in Orlando. He always bragged that it was a long barrel, full-choke gun. I was proud that Ray let me have it, and someday it will belong to one of you boys.

Although my father and mother were separated, we regained contact with my mother after about twenty years subsequent to me being discharged from the Navy. We visited her many times during her remaining years in Fort Lauderdale, Florida, along with our wonderful stepfather, Harold Ormston. When she passed away on September 3, 1986, we received some jewelry and a few other items of interest but not of much value. However, when Harold passed away, we received an equal share of her estate, which was a good sum for each of her thirteen heirs.

TELL ME A STORY ABOUT OUR FAMILY, PAPA

I have told you much about my family in all the previous sections of this book. I will also tell you some short stories at the end of this book about certain ones in our family. I may not cover all of them, but there are at least a few of them.

I will give you a brief statement about my great-grandfather, my grandfather's dad, Reacie Layton John Thomas Eldridge. He moved from Dooley County, Georgia, to Colquitt County, Georgia, in the early 1900s with his family. He was an Independent Baptist preacher, and he preached in several of the older churches in Colquitt County, Georgia, including some Methodist churches. The information I received from my grandfather is that he was a great person to pattern one's self by. He died on December 30, 1929, and is buried in the Hopewell Baptist Church cemetery near our farm. I have very little information about our great-grandmother, Ann Nipper; however, I do have a photo of her. She and Reacie had eleven children. After Ann's death, Reacie married Liza Jane Walker Huff, who had three children of her own, and then they had four children: Effie, Evie, Sally, and William.

My grandfather, Homer, was also a great man and very kind to his grandchildren; and all of us loved him very much. He attended to us after our parents separated and our father was looking for a new wife to help care for his children. He would do anything for us and us him. He worked very hard even when times were tough and there were no jobs during the Great Depression. He stayed in Orlando after we moved to Georgia since he had so many friends there. My family and I visited him in Orlando and went to church with him when we could. I have photos of him with Larry (Gramps) and Aunt Lynn when they were very young. I was visiting him when he became ill and passed away on June 21, 1967. He is buried in the Sardis Primitive Baptist Church cemetery. I have very little information about my grandmother Lelia Eldridge except that she died in 1916 and is buried in Worth County, Georgia, near Ashburn, Georgia. Leila was Granddaddy's third cousin, and that was my dad's mother. Granddaddy later married Belle Keene in 1919, and they had four children: Rebecca, Juanita, Quinton, and Pansy. Ms. Belle died a short time after the last child was born, and that left my grandfather with five children to support. He could not accomplish this task; so he put three of them (Rebecca, Juanita, and Quinton) in an orphanage in DeLand, Florida. Aunt Pansy (my dad's sister) went to live with our aunt Willie Eldridge Cannon (Granddaddy's sister) in Sigsbee, Georgia, and was raised by her until she married Uncle Charlie B. Meadows. Sigsbee is a small community north of Moultrie.

WHERE DO YOU KEEP PHOTOGRAPHS OR IMAGES FROM YOUR LIFETIME?

I have boxes of photos located in our closet in Georgia that are not displayed. I have photos of all our family members, including your mother while she was growing up. I also kept many of their papers, drawings, and miscellaneous artifacts that they did in grammar school and afterward. I also have many photos of my siblings and their children and many other photos of my aunts, uncles, and cousins taken during our family reunions and at parties or family gatherings. My military photos are also located with these.

WHAT IS YOUR FAVORITE PHOTOGRAPH?

That is an easy one. It absolutely has to be the ones of Mema's and my wedding. I can look at them and see how things were in 1953 and compare the photos to our families today, the ones that are living. Many of our relatives and friends have passed away. All of Mema's family that was at our wedding, except her siblings, have passed away.

DID YOU EVER KEEP A JOURNAL? WHAT DID YOU LIKE TO RECORD?

I never kept a journal because it took too much time and organization, sorry about that. Mema and I destroyed all our old love letters because we did not want to embarrass any of you boys with all that LOVE stuff. It remains in our hearts, and that is all that matters.

However, I was one to keep track of all our activities such as doctor's appointments and things of that nature. I carried a small book in my shirt pocket and noted any major happenings or events. These books were very important to Mema and me as we needed reminders for our plans and personal transactions. These books were filed away with my income tax records each year. My military records are like a journal in a way; each time I was assigned to a squadron or went on military training, I had written orders detailing exactly the functions of this period of time. These records are filed in my office.

MEMORIES ARE SPECIAL FAMILY TREASURES

WHAT MEMORIES ABOUT YOUR PARENTS, CHILDREN, AND LIFE DO YOU WANT TO SHARE WITH ME?

My memories span from when I was about three years old until our present time. My grandfather worked for the WPA during the lean years of our economy. I remember going with him when he worked on the highway department in Orlando. His job was to hang lanterns on the road construction barricades. In the morning, he would collect the lanterns and remove the globes for cleaning. Once he cleaned the globes, he would reinstall them and fill the lanterns with fuel as this was the power source for lighting the barricades. In the evening, he would return to his job and hang the lanterns on the barricades for illumination. This was to be done each morning and each evening for the safety of the road construction.

My dad was a very hard worker but had time to care for us in the evenings. It was normal for him to take all his family to the movies several times each week while we were in Orlando. He would also spend time helping the Salvation Army during their programs for helping many children in the neighborhood that were less fortunate than we were. He would distribute candy and toys to many children, and that would make him happy that he could do that for them. I have many memories of my summers in Georgia. When school was out for the summer, Daddy would bring my sister, Aunt Betty, and me to Georgia for the summer. We would spend time at various relatives' homes and help with the chores as needed. We would spend time at Uncle Clarence and Aunt Sally Mims', Uncle Artie and Aunt Evie Tompkins', and Uncle Butler and Aunt Clydie Mae Gays'. They would treat us as their own, and each of them would see that we were taken care of as one of their own. I grew up with all the children of these families and remained close to each of them for many years. It saddens me to realize that many of my dear cousins have passed away and some of them were much younger than me.

Another good memory is of our family traveling to Georgia for a short visit to the same families. Uncle Artie would put Gene and me in the bedroom with four of his boys, and they normally slept in the buff. Now that was a change for this ole modest boy. There would be three boys per bed as there were only two beds per room. Aunt Betty would sleep with the other girls, and Pat would sleep with Daddy. We had a great time on these trips, and it made us closer to our Georgia families. However, it was always an eventful occasion while riding to and from Georgia. There would be four boys in the back seat, and Betty would ride in the front seat with Daddy and our stepmother. One time, Daddy hit a bump in the road and jarred us boys in the back seat. Thinking that I had hit him, Uncle Gene whacked me one in retaliation for the bump. Another memorable time was when Daddy missed a critical turn in one of the small towns. He drove several miles and then realized that he had made an incorrect turn miles back. Instead of turning back, he continued on until he came to a small wooden bridge that was in need of repairs very badly. Daddy got out of the car and walked the length of the entire bridge to ensure that it was safe enough for him to proceed on. We made it across and went on our merry way as if nothing had happened.

As mentioned previously, we were very close to our cousins who lived down the road from us, the Tompkins. During the summer, we would work together in the tobacco fields or cotton fields and get very dirty. When our day's work was done, Daddy would allow us to go swimming with the Tompkins children in our favorite wash hole down the road. We called it Chapman's Wash Hole. Once there, we would all take off our clothes and swim in our birthday suits (or some call it naked). We made a swing in one of the trees and utilized it for our big splash in the deeper part of the wash hole. Once while we were swimming in the hole, the girls from a nearby home paid us a visit. I guess you know that most all of us stayed in the water so we would not give away any secrets, except Uncle Gene and his friend, Billy Flowers; they exposed themselves to God and everybody. The girls did not tarry very long because they had already seen more than they bargained for. This was great fun, and we talk of these episode many times when we gather for reunions or funerals.

My mother, Anna Melinda Hodge Eldridge, was born to Augustus F. and Lizzie Thompson Hodge on September 10, 1915, in Danville, Georgia. After my mother, Anna Malinda Hodge Eldridge, divorced my dad, she wandered to several places until she settled in Key West, Florida. There she met and married a Navy chief named Harold Ormston. He was our stepfather and was a prince of a man to all his stepchildren. He was very good to my mother, but they never had any children of their own; however, he treated us as his own and loved our children as his own. When he was discharged from the Navy with about thirty years of service, they moved to Fort Lauderdale, Florida, and lived in their home until my mother died on September 3, 1986. Dad Ormston moved to an apartment for a while; and then he moved to Orange Park, Florida, to be near us so we could care for him as he was failing in health. He lived there several years until he died October 15, 1992, and was buried at sea as he wished.

Mema's parents (your great-great-grandparents), Wheeler (JW) and Ola Norman, were a very special part our life. Before Mema and I married, we would sit on a couch in the living room and talk. One evening we were sitting there, and her father walked in to tell her it was time for supper. Well, I had my arm on the back of the couch, but it was not touching Mema at all. When they left the room, he asked her, "You're getting sort of chummy, aren't you?" And Mema replied to him in a nice way that there was nothing to it. After Mema and I were married, her parents took me in as one of their very own and treated me very special. Since I did not associate with my parents, it was very special that Mema's parents treated me so special. I would go many places with Dad and especially to our many churches in South Georgia. I would help them work whenever Mema and I visited on many occasions, whether we lived here or in Florida. Mom and Dad were so very generous to Mema, Larry (Gramps), Aunt Lynn, and me during the times we lived with them and also when we would visit from Florida. They would always pack a sack with meat and other things for us to take home. They were also generous to many of the preachers in this area as they would give them lots of things during the year and especially on the holidays. Dad would butcher turkeys before Thanksgiving and take them to preachers in the area as well as some of his homemade syrup. Mom and Dad knew many people in Colquitt County and the surrounding counties as they attended many churches in Georgia and Florida. Dad did not have very much formal education; however, he could do most anything he wanted in the line of construction on the farm.

He was a master at making syrup in the old-fashioned way, cooking it in a kettle and later in an evaporator. He would cook syrup from before sunup until dark for many weeks. It was the best syrup in the country, and people would come from all over the country to purchase his syrup. When he purchased the farm that we currently live on, it was nothing but a lot of trees and tree stumps, and it did not have a pond. Dad Norman removed all the trees and stumps from the land that he wanted to farm. It was hard labor, but he was determined to make a good farm; and he did. Enough can't be said about his willpower and determination to accomplish the thing that he dreamed of doing or the things that he wanted. Mom and Dad Norman were very generous to Sardis Church and were members from the annual meeting on September 25, 1954, until each of them passed away—Dad on March 6, 1987, and Mom on January 5, 1997. Dad built the house in 1942 that Mema and I occupy on 2303 Sardis Church Road and did it almost by himself. He taught Larry (Gramps) how to fish, hunt, and attend to cows and hogs. He would do lots of the surgical procedures on his animals and even sew them up when completed. Larry would always help his grandpa do many of the chores and even operate on hogs from time to time.

Grandpa would let Larry drive his tractors and pull wagons wherever he directed him to do so. Larry and Lynn were always very good children while growing up, and Mema and I made sure of that. Mema and I believed in having them do the things that we thought they should and corrected them if they did not. Larry and Lynn behaved very well in church and when we were with other people. They were both very generous to children in our neighborhood when they had candy or other things to give away. It seemed that there were always some children in our yard playing or just hanging around. Each of them enjoyed their time in the Scouts and participated until it got to be boring for them. Both of them were in the Clay High band, Lynn played the clarinet and Larry the percussion instruments.

Larry (Gramps) and Aunt Lynn both joined the Navy while I was a recruiting officer and stayed in the reserves for several years. Larry was in the Seabees, a construction unit, and went on active duty several times and seemed to enjoy his affiliation until he was injured and was released from duty. Aunt Lynn was in the supply corps and went on active duty as well; and on one active duty tour, she went to Rota, Spain, where she had a special time with some of my Navy friends that were stationed there and previously stationed with me at Jacksonville.

Larry (Gramps) was a lot like some of you boys in that he would like to daydream in school after returning from a visit to the farm on weekends. He was much worse after summer was over and school started. He missed his Grandpa Norman very much and would have rather been with him on the farm. When we lived in one of Grandpa's houses on the Cannon farm, Larry would hide in his car so he could go home with him. We would see Larry hiding in the back but said nothing about it because Grandpa did not mind. Grandpa would drive off, and we would follow in a few minutes; and by the time we arrived, Grandma would have dinner ready. Grandpa was almost as easy on Larry as we are on our boys; I guess it's an inherited thing, huh?

After graduating from high school, Larry went to Key West and stayed with Aunt Betty and Uncle Jabe, her first husband. He, Greg, and Gary (Aunt Betty's sons) were like the Three Musketeers as they did a lot of activities together such as cleaning boats and selling fish. I know that it was a lot of fun, but all good things must come to an end; so we told him that he must come home and get a paying and responsible job. He went to work at the Winn-Dixie warehouse for a short time but did not like it there very much; therefore, when Mema and I had traveled to California for a Naval conference, he quit and went to the farm to help Grandpa Norman and Uncle Herman work. Grandpa paid him $25 per week and let him stay with them for free (room and board). That did not last very long, so he then started working for the Chevrolet dealer in Moultrie. Larry had done very well in auto mechanics in high school and went on to upgrade competition in Orlando, Florida, where he finished in the top group of the competition.

He had not worked at the dealership very long before he caught the eye of this pretty, sweet, little bashful girl from Berlin, Marsha Bell. Larry sort of thought that Marsha was cute and started flirting with her by moving her time card from place to place so it was difficult for her to find. She soon caught on to what he was doing, and they have been together ever since. They would spend a lot of their dates sitting on Grandma's couch watching TV under the watchful eye of Grandpa, Grandma, and Uncle Lincoln. Larry eventually had enough nerve to ask the other one about marriage, and they were married on February 26, 1977. The rest is history.

Not surprising to anyone, they went to Key West on their honeymoon. Diana was born on December 11, 1977. Later they moved to Orange Park and lived with us until we built them a home on Morgan Circle Drive. Larry worked at Kmart for about six months and then was hired at the Naval air depot to work on aircraft. Larry worked for the Navy until he retired in September 2011. However, during this time, he and Marsha helped me with our construction company building custom homes and installing roofs. Larry was a certified roofer for a while and assisted me in our roofing operations and doing whatever he needed to do to help on the construction of our custom home building. Larry would spray-paint whenever needed and haul supplies as well. Larry was a great worker for the Navy and eventually was promoted to a good position in his department where he remained until his retirement. He was extremely versed in writing contracts for the Navy ships repairs at Mayport Naval Station near Jacksonville, Florida. After retirement, he went back to work as a contractor for the same division.

After working for me in the construction business, Grammie worked for several other construction corporations and golf-course corporations as their controller, vice president / director of finance and human resources. However, Grammie says her best job of all is being a mommy to your mommies (Diana and Lisa) and a grammie to you four boys: Christopher, Bradley, Cameron, and Blake.

To keep Diana occupied and to have someone to make sandwiches for her, Lisa was born on September 20, 1982, and that completed their little family except for our precious angel that we lost on May 6, 1985, Christina, who is buried in Sardis Church Cemetery in Colquitt County near Moultrie, Georgia. We always enjoyed Diana and Lisa as they grew from our little "boys" to beautiful young ladies whom we were always proud to have as our granddaughters. It is impossible for me to write about all my memories of them while they were growing up. Diana lived with Mema and me for at least a year two different times, and Lisa lived with us for a year one time; so we had a lot of time to spoil them like we do you boys. Both were very talented in their own way. I will tell you a couple of things that stand out in my mind, but I do not have enough time nor paper to tell you all I remember about my two little darlings.

Aunt Lynn had a full schedule in high school as she was lead clarinet in the band and was very good at her position. They did a lot of competing and brought home the trophies for Clay High School on many occasions. Aunt Lynn was pretty popular in high school and was well-liked by most of her classmates. After graduation, she went to work at Winn-Dixie headquarters and loved her job in the Monterey department. Eventually, she would apply for a civil service position at the personnel department at the Naval air station and was selected in a short time. She worked in many divisions of the department and did well in each of them as Aunt Lynn is a fast learner and is very well organized in her work. She applied to go overseas to Guantanamo Bay, Cuba, and was selected for a position in the personnel department. She remained in this position for over six years and loved the area and work. During her deployment, each one of her family went to visit her and enjoyed the relax atmosphere in that area. On one trip, Mema and Papa took Uncle Gene and Aunt Mary with them as they had never been to the island. Once her tour of duty was ended in Gitmo, Aunt Lynn was transferred to Millington Naval Base near Memphis, Tennessee, where she stayed for three years. On her way to Memphis, she stopped by to visit Mema and Papa for a short time. Papa had a quadruple heart bypass in Tallahassee, Florida; so she wanted to be there at that time. She had always worked for the Aviation Navy, but in Memphis, she worked for the shipboard sailors and loved it. She grew tired of being over there by herself, so she transferred to DCMA in Saint Augustine, Florida, where she has done very well for herself in being promoted to a high-level position and a great deal of responsibility. Papa built her a home on the same tract of land that he built Gramps' and Grammy's on, and they can look out for one another.

This is a short story on my "boys." Diana went with me to take the trash to our old landfill, and on one occasion I mentioned about some of the people being so "inconsiderate" about putting their trash on the side of the road instead of taking it to the dumpster. On the next trip, we were riding down the old dirt road, and there was lots of trash on each side of the road. Diana said, "Papa, these people sure are inconsiderate, aren't they?"

I answered, "They sure are," and was surprised that she remembered that word at her young age; she was about five years old at the time.

Lisa was riding with me one day going across the Buckman Bridge to look at a repair job, and she asked me a question. I do not remember the question, but after giving her a detailed explanation, she looked over at me and said so earnestly, "Papa, I don't believe boys," and didn't even crack a smile. When Lisa was about four years old, Diana would ask her to prepare her a sandwich because Diana did not know how. Lisa would put peanut butter and jelly on a slice of bread and top it off with potato chips. What a combination! However, Diana would eat it every time.

Short Stories of Our Family
That You May Like

A TESTIMONY OF HOW GOD CARES AND PROTECTS US FROM HARM

Note: it is written, "Ye shall not tempt the Lord your God." Another commitment was written as "He will never leave you nor forsake you." These statements are sure and steadfast, as the Lord has written. This is a true story that has never been told to anyone, not even Mema.

In the summer of 2014, I contracted with Mr. Jodie Hart to convert his old cow barn into a suitable living and entertaining facility. While renovating this building, I witnessed firsthand the blessings and protection of our Lord and Savior.

My crew and I were using a large pneumatic nail gun that shoots three-and-one-half-inch nails into large pieces of board to frame the interior of the building. Two of my men were in the ceiling framing the structure with one of these guns while I was standing below directing the operation as I wanted it accomplished.

On one occasion, I was below when I directed the men using the gun to "shoot right here." When the man pulled the trigger, the end of the gun missed the spot, and the large nail was flying down toward my face as I was standing below looking upward. The nail normally propels point down as to anchor two boards together. On this occasion, the nail flipped and propelled straight at my face; however, it tipped another object on the way down. The flat part came down first, so I did not receive the full impact of the force. In a frantic mode, I knew the nail was going to strike me in the face, and there was nothing I could do to move out of the way. This nail came at a high rate of speed toward my face and hit me in the upper lip as I tried to dodge out of the way. I knew that I had been injured as blood was coming from my mouth and my lip; however, I did not know the extent of damage. I could envision my upper lip being anchored to my lower lip as that is what would normally occur in this situation. As it hit me, I screamed "O Lord, no," as I instantly thought I had been struck by the sharp end and imagined the worst. It did hurt with severe pain as it tore into my upper lip and the pressure penetrated through my lip and broke my upper denture. I was frantic, as were the two other men. We examined my face, lip, and dentures and determined that I had been spared the severe damage as the Lord would have it. I backed off and started feeling my lip to determine the extent of damage. Both men jumped down from the ceiling and were in a panic mode as well.

Although I was in pain, I determined that the extent of damage was not as bad as I had suspected previously.

I was bleeding from the gash in my upper lip, and it had begun to swell. I then expressed my gratitude to my Lord for protecting me from extensive damage and taking care of me in a stupid act. I was very relieved when all went as well as it did in this dangerous situation.

Long story short, our Lord will look out for all His children, as it is written in many places in the Bible. When I came home that night, Mema inquired as to why my lip was bleeding a little and swollen. I explained to her that I had been hit with a board, which was a normal occurrence in our business. My little white lie saved me from being chastised severely by her, which was okay.

MY DADDY'S VISIT TO TOWN

One day my granddaddy (your great-great-great-grandfather) was going to town in a horse-drawn wagon, and my daddy wanted to go along with him. Granddaddy explained to Daddy that he must remain in the wagon while he did some shopping, so Daddy agreed to that. Upon arriving in town, Granddaddy told Daddy to sit there like a good child and not say anything to anyone because they might think that Daddy was a fool. As it went, Daddy was sitting there minding his own business when a man approached him and started talking to him. Daddy would not say anything to him because of the warning he had from Granddaddy. The man tried to get Daddy to talk to him and offered him an apple to do so; however, Daddy, being the obedient boy that he was, still refused to talk to the man. Being kind of disgusted, the man looked at Daddy and said, "You must be a darn fool," and then he walked away. After a while, Granddaddy came back to the wagon. Daddy had to tell him about the man. He told Granddaddy that the man found out that he was "a darn fool," and he did not even open his mouth. I guess the moral of this story is, "Sometimes you do not have to open your mouth for someone to find out that you are a darn fool!" Be careful what you say and how you say it.

DRESSED GEESE

Mema's father, Wheeler Norman, your great-great-grandfather, made homemade syrup each year from sugarcane. He would grind the sugarcane and cook the cane juice in a large vat until it was processed into syrup. In doing this, he would remove the impurities from the juice by skimming it from the top of the cane juice, which floated to the top as it cooked. These skimming would be put in a large barrel to be disposed of at a later time. While the skimming remained in the barrel, it would ferment and become wine or an alcoholic liquid. One day your great-great-grandfather poured this liquid into a hole for disposing of it. Later, he noticed that several of his geese were lying on the ground as if they were dead and not moving any. Not wanting to waste anything, he pulled the feathers off the geese and threw them in an area near our pond. The next morning, all the geese were in his backyard naked as a jaybird. They had become drunk on the cane skimmings, and he thought they were dead. This was not good since it was wintertime and they needed some protection from the cold weather. Your great-great-grandmother (Ola Norman) made outfits for each of the naked geese so they would be warm. This story was verified by several of your kinfolk to Mema and me.

THE LAST MORNING

by Diana Eldridge Warren

1997

●━━━●━━━●

Note: Subsequent to an emergency trip to the hospital and the hospital staff doing everything in their power, Mema's mother, Mrs. Ola Mae McMullen Norman, passed away on January 5, 1997. This was a devastating blow to all of us that tended to her for several years. As indicated by the writer of the below letter, many of her near kin and several of her so-called close relatives had not visited her in several weeks or months. Mom was such a lovely and caring person, and she would have loved our boys as she did their mothers. This is your great-great-grandmother.

On the gloomy Sunday morning of January 5, 1997, I entered the back entrance of the Colquitt County Hospital, knowing that I was about to see the face of my great-grandmother for one of the last times for she had just passed away. This had to be one of the most tragic mornings of my life. As we reached the fourth floor, I became very, almost to a panic state. I didn't know if I could handle seeing her this way or not.

Finally, we approached the room. Outside I saw some of my other relatives standing around crying. I had a really hard time understanding why some of them seemed so upset, for they had not come to see Grandma in so long. I knew they couldn't possibly be as heartbroken as I was. Then I entered the room to see her lying there in the bed the same way I had seen her only hours before. This time she wasn't struggling for a breath or wrinkling her forehead because of the pain. She just lay there in total peace for now she had gone to be with her Father in heaven.

THE SISTER I WILL NEVER KNOW

by Lisa Eldridge
November 13, 1999

———•——•——•———

Note: The below poem was written by Lisa Eldridge about the death of her sister, Christina, who was delivered on May 6, 1985. Grammie had carried her for six months, and an examination determined that she had died the night before. It was such a tragic loss to all of us, and we still mourn her loss as if it was yesterday. Lisa was almost three years old when Christina was born, but she evidently thought of her a lot and, in her own way, mourned her loss. Lisa was twelve years old when she wrote this letter to her beloved sister one day on the way from Orange Park, Florida, to Moultrie, Georgia, to visit her great-great-grandmother.

When I think of my life and the things I have done
I wonder about how things would be if you were here
We could have played with our Barbies
I could have been the teacher
And you could have been the student
Whenever we played school

You could have told me your secrets
And I wouldn't think about spilling a word
I could have told you a thing or two about soccer and boys

I could have helped you get ready for your prom
Or maybe even for your wedding

I still don't understand why it has to be the way it is
I have so many questions like:
What would you have looked like?
What would your interest be in music, clothes, and boys?
What kind of choices would you have made?
Would your life turn out the way you wanted it too?
The memories we could have shared
But you are the sister I will never know
Who I often think of

I will never have to worry about you because you are up above,
Hand in hand with God looking down on us
Now we all gather here, as we bring you home
And one day, when that one day comes
When we will meet
When I come home

UNCLE JACK'S WORLD WAR II STORY

⎯⎯⎯•⎯⎯⎯•⎯⎯⎯

During World War II we fought Germany and Japan. Germany invaded our friends in Europe, and Japan invaded our county in Pearl Harbor on December 7, 1941. They killed many of our soldiers and sailors in this bombing and destroyed many of our planes and ships. Our president, Franklin D. Roosevelt, declared war on Japan for this aggression; and we had thousands of our military killed and many more wounded in this war.

Your uncle Jack Burke, Aunt Betty's second husband, flew as a tail gunner in one of our largest bombers at this time, a B-24. This is the same aircraft that Papa flew in while he was in the Navy. This aircraft had twelve crew members that had various functions to accomplish its mission. On one of these flight missions Uncle Jack knew that the aircraft had been hit by Japanese guns many times but could not observe the damage from his position in the tail of the aircraft. Upon their return to the base, they had to be escorted in landing their aircraft as it was damaged extensively. Subsequent to landing, Uncle Jack dismounted from the aircraft to learn that he and the pilot were the only survivors of that ill-fated flight. All his buddies were killed in this one flight except the pilot, which was a blessing within itself as he is the one that directs the aircraft in all operations. We were all blessed to know Uncle Jack as he was a true patriot to the United States of America and to all veterans regardless of their branch of military service. He later joined the Navy where he served the remainder of his military career and retired.

MY SISTER AND MY BROTHERS

As I have previously mentioned, my sister and brothers have always had a great rapport with one another throughout our entire life. Yes, we have had our differences, but nothing we couldn't reconcile. As youngsters, we played together a lot and had a wonderful time doing so. As each of us graduated from high school and left home to make our fortune, we sort of made our own niche in life and had our own little families. Each of us remained in contact with one another with all our special events that happened, and in some cases, we attended one another's special occasions such as the birth of our children, weddings, and on a couple of sad occasions, funerals.

In our latter years, we grew closer to one another as we felt that we needed one another's support and comfort in certain times. Many of our friends would watch with amazement at how much we stayed in contact with one another and shared our many events in life, such as the birth of our children, grandchildren, and more especially, the birth of our great-grandchildren. Each of us would brag about our little ones as if there were no other children in the world that could do what ours could.

At the present time (June 19, 2017) my sister, Aunt Betty, lives in Shallotte, North Carolina; and she comes to visit us one or two times a year, and we try to visit her in the fall of each year. My brother Uncle Pat and his wife, Aunt Clarice, live in Orange Park, Florida. Uncle Gene and Aunt Mary live in an assisted-living facility near Orange Park, Florida. Uncle Gene and Aunt Mary had to move here after an accident left them unable to care for themselves. A lot of times, something good generates from a tragedy. Uncle Gene's accident caused him to move here, and that made it possible for Uncle Pat and me to assist him and Aunt Mary and visit much more than we could when they lived in Colorado. Two of my last three brothers were half brothers. This means that we had the same father but different mothers. The other brother was a stepbrother. My stepmother had been married previously, and this child was from that marriage. We were all raised as brothers and sister. My youngest half brother, Charlie Ray, still lives on the old farm Daddy purchased in 1945. He and his daughter, Amanda, and her husband, Charlie Hamilton, live in our old home across the road from Ray. Ray was a mechanic all his life and retired in 2016 to enjoy time with his family. My other half brother, Kenneth Lavon, passed away on January 6, 2016, from complications of surgery. My only stepbrother, James Leonard Hart Jr., also known as JL, died on December 27, 2004, from a self-inflicted gunshot wound in his home in Moultrie.

As I attempt to finish your book, I realize that all of us are getting older, and according to time, we do not have a great deal of time left on this old earth. Our time has been extremely rewarding as we have a great family to carry on our tradition and our wishes, as we have done through all our years. It is my prayer that I have done something to assist in developing the minds, souls, and bodies of my great family. I have always stated that I would consider myself a success in life if I could have my children, grandchildren, and great-grandchildren love me as I did my grandfather, Homer Eldridge. In the past years, I feel that I have reached that goal from the actions and interactions of my family. It is so good to be loved; however, one must earn this respect as it is not given to everyone.

A STORY ABOUT A LADY

by Homer (Papa) Eldridge

LADY
September 11, 1996

Hello, my name is Lady. At least it is now. I was born around June 1984 and am a combination of French poodle and, I think, Pekingese. I do not know exactly what my father was because I do not remember him very well. To the best of recollection, I didn't have such a good life for the first year. I can't remember a whole lot about it, but I must not have been in a good home because my owners took me out to Sardis Church Road and dumped me to the mercies of the world and all those country elements. This was sometime in either late June or early July of 1985. As the tale goes, I wandered up to the home of Mrs. Ola Norman one Sunday afternoon, and I saw a lot of people standing around saying goodbye to one another and just generally talking. They seemed to be pretty nice folks, and I came up to the house looking for something to eat. I remember thinking that it sure would be nice if I could get something from these people. As this group started making talk about me and how bad I looked, I remember this older lady saying something about getting "this little puppy something to eat." Now that was my kind of woman.

There was a lot of discussion about many things, and during this time, these people discussed everything from taking me someplace else or just getting rid of me anyway. However, in all this discussion and evaluation, it was determined by the older guy, I believe his name was Papa, that I could stay for at least a little while. I was fed and put in a good place by the other older guy named Lincoln.

I learned later on that this guy was a good friend to have because he always made sure that I had plenty of food and water in my bowls. Yeah, I now had a bowl for water and a bowl for food. I thought to myself, *I think I'm going to like this place even if that big crowd did leave.* Everything remained real good for about week or so, and I sort of got into a routine.

I believe it was the middle of the next week when these two ladies that were part of the big crowd came back to the farm, and they brought two of the cutest little girls with them, Diana and Lisa, I believe. Now they were with them on our previous meeting; but their parents, Larry and Marsha, wouldn't let them get near me because of my odor and looks. I believe I heard some discussion about me remaining but that I had to get some shots, a bath, and something about a "fixin'." I learned later that this "fixin'" was to adjust my internal affairs so I could not have any puppies or have the desire to want any. This was not a good week for me, but I survived. When I came home from the beauty shop, I thought I was something else, and I really looked like something else other than when I came to this home.

I kept waiting for something to happen to me, but these people were treating me real good. And I sensed on occasions that they even thought I was cute. Someone, I believe it was Marsha, the mother of the two little girls, named me Lady. I thought after this that I must be going to stay around if they were giving me a name. This gave me a little more secure feeling, and I began to take things as they came for a while. That weekend, the rest of the crowd came back, and you have never seen so much huggin' and kissin' in all your life. I thought for a minute that my turn was coming up next, but thank goodness, it never did.

After the weekend was over and all these people began huggin' and kissin' again to say goodbye to Grandma and Grandpa Norman, I thought maybe that I would be left alone for another spell. I was wrong. They put me in their car and took me to their home in Orange Park, Florida, wherever that is. It was a nice place, but it wasn't like Grandma's. For the next few years, we did travel a lot; I began to enjoy this because these were really nice people, and they took care of me like I was one of the girls. Diana and Lisa played with me a lot when they weren't playing with Muffin, the darned ole cat that had taken up at their house previously. I found out later that she had been "fixed" also, so that made me feel that these people were not prejudiced to certain animals. Muffin and I didn't always see eye to eye, but we got along pretty good until the girls came messing around with us and wanting to hug and kiss us like those Georgia folks did.

Time went on, and everything went along well. Everyone was busy doing their thing and trying to stay busy. I must say that was a busy family. They were always doing something: working at the base, building houses, playing Navy, going for supplies, and running all over town for Papa. He was the boss (he thought). I even went to Disney World a time or two. During the day I would stay in this pen, but in the afternoon my family would come get me so I could guard them during the night. I would even sleep in the RV with them and, boy, could some of them snore. Not only did I go to Disney but I also went almost everywhere with them. I guess it was because they were scared and needed a watchdog along, the only thing I could think of.

As the years went by, a lot of things happened to this family, both good and bad; however, they always stood by one another no matter what took place. I put on a little weight and was not able to do the things I was used to doing, but once in a while, someone would help me up on the couch or in my chair. Yes, my chair. I had a certain chair that I slept in (snored in) at Mems and Papa's unless I wanted peace and quiet, then I would go someplace else to rest. I'm staying in Georgia more now that everyone in Orange Park is busy. I really like it up here. I'm basically my own boss and am not disturbed like I am in Orange Park. The girls were always fussing over me and making me talk ugly to them. If they could only know what I was saying to them, they would leave me alone. I do enjoy sleeping with them in the wintertime because it makes me so warm, but I just wish they would leave me alone. Mema and Papa have me spoiled a little bit also, but not like Grandma did. I really miss her not being around. She died on January 6, 1997, and they said something about her going to be with the Lord, whoever he is. I know she's happy because she said after Grandpa died that she would rather be with him. Maybe everything worked out for them. I hope so because they sure were wonderful people and really knew how to take care of animals. Grandma would pull chicken off the bone for me, and I would eat until she would feed me no more. She sure had a way with making sure everyone had enough food to eat and water to drink.

Over the years we have had several other animals share the house with us. I guess the best one was Muffin, the old cat. She got real sick last month, and the family had to have her put to sleep. We all still miss her, but maybe Lisa misses her the most. Lisa made her a flower arrangement and put it on her grave in the backyard. It just doesn't seem the same without her being around, but life must go on. Now there was a large black-and-white dog that belonged to Diana. This dog would not let anyone rest and was always into mischief. Something happened to this dog, and she could not be cured either. She also is buried in the backyard near Muffin. From the way I see things, when I die, I guess the family will put me in the backyard also. I hope it's not next to Taylor because I never did get along well with that dog. Before Aunt Lynn was transferred to Gitmo Bay, Cuba, she had to find a home for her little cat. I heard the conversation about letting it stay with us, and it didn't interest me one bit. That would be two cats in one house; I would never get anything to eat anymore. I could hear them talking, but I couldn't get my two cents' worth in at all. This was going to be a disaster. That cat's name is Mitten, and she is also "fixed," ha.

I can't believe how fast Diana and Lisa are growing up. Diana will be twenty-one on December 11, and Lisa will be sweet sixteen (and never been kissed, huh) in a few days, September 20. These "boys" (I do not know why Papa calls them boys) are very busy with their lives, and between the two of them, they are into everything. I heard Mema and Papa talking the other night, and Lisa has done got her a job as a cheerleader, "What else is that girl going to do?" I saw her carrying a camera around the other day, and she said something about being a photographer for the school events. I believe she is taking those pictures for the yearbook, whatever that is. I think she is going through the phase Diana went through, looking at the boys more and more. I sure hope she doesn't bring one like the last one

Diana brought home. That guy was something else, but I must say he had an eye for me. I wonder if he paid attention to me to get on the good side of Diana because he knew how she couldn't resist me and my lovable disposition. Some guys will try anything to get in good with a girl.

It seems that I am getting to the point where I cannot see or hear very well anymore, but sometimes that's to my advantage. I just walk around minding my own business, mostly outside because Mema gets mad when I do my "business" in the house. I love to lie in the sand in the sunshine, but fleas are terrible during the summer. When I get to looking real bad and needing a haircut, Papa will take me to Debbie's Salon. That lady really knows how to make a person feel good and look good. I can't say too much about her pens though, and the company I have to put up with while I am there is terrible. When I get home from the beauty shop, everyone makes over me and talks about how good I look. I do look good, and I strut my stuff too. Debbie dresses me to the tee with a neckerchief, paints my toenails, and puts a bow in my hair. I really do look tough!

I guess we're going to Orange Park this weekend as I heard Papa telling Marsha to look for us Sunday afternoon. I enjoy riding with Mema and Papa. They put me on a blanket in the rear seat and have me a cup of water on the floor, just in case I get thirsty. They really know how to treat a lady.

DO NOT EVER, EVER QUIT

This is a story about perseverance and determination. Of course, it is not a true story but one only to get my point across about staying the course and being determined to succeed on your own. Don't let anyone deter you nor persuade you from your main goal in life as you wish it to be. This story illustrates determination: One day a farmer left a pail of milk in the barn unattended. After a while, two frogs came along and jumped upon the edge of the pail and fell in. Both frogs knew that unless someone came along and pulled them out, they were doomed. They started kicking and splashing for a long time, and finally, one of the frogs told the other one that he was very tired and he wasn't going to kick anymore. So he drowned.

The other frog just kept on kicking and splashing in hopes that he would be saved from drowning. After a while, the farmer came back to get the milk and saw the two frogs in his milk, one was dead and the other one was lying on top of a clump of butter asleep.

You must realize that splashing and churning milk eventually makes butter. The moral of this story is do not EVER, EVER quit when you have a goal in life for your success. Some will try to persuade you to do different, but stay on course and your dreams will come true. I will not tell you that there will not be sacrifices along the way, but the grand reward will be YOURS.

HOW I MET YOUR GREAT-GRANDMOTHER

written by Papahe

———•———•———

I was dating Mema's cousin, a nice young chick named Carolyn Joyner (aka the Chicken Lady). They decided that they should go on a double date and make the evening more interesting. Carolyn arranged for Mema to go out with a young man with the last name of Taylor. I knew him from being around him in church and other social gatherings, and he was a nice guy.

I had the car, so I drove around and picked everyone up for our evening of excitement. I guess we went to the drive-in movie, and I started paying more attention to Mema as the evening progressed. We discussed several things and got more acquainted as the evening passed.

I was the only one that was a senior in high school, and during the course of the evening, Mema asked to see my class ring. I do not know what prompted me to give my class ring to a young girl that I had only met a few hours prior to that; however, I did.

After all the fun was over and our time with the girls had expired, I took the Taylor guy home first as Carolyn was spending the night with Mema. I expressed to them how much I had enjoyed the evening and told them that I would see them later. For some unknown reason, Mema kept my class ring and put it on a chain around her neck. That was the custom back in the old days.

I knew that I had to get my ring back so my parents would not think that I had lost it. I made arrangements to meet Mema at a special period of music appreciation held in the auditorium. If my memory serves me correct, she had already put tape on my ring so that she could wear it on one of her fingers versus wearing it on her neck. I presume she asked me if she could keep it for a while, and I know that I agreed to let her do so. Now this was a girl that I had only met a day or so ago and knew nothing about at all. However, I knew I would like to see more of her; but I was a bashful guy, and I didn't have all the confidence that I have now.

Here was this beautiful green-eyed brunette with all the curves in the right places, and she was paying attention to me, a fellow with an inferiority complex that would not quit. However, I liked the attention very much. This girl had been the Colquitt County beauty queen for two years, and she could actually date any of many boys in school with better credentials than I had; but she chose me. The Lord had to be in this matter, and I know that now; but I was oblivious of it then. At this point, our hearts were well connected, and little things started happening that we could not explain. I met Mema's large immediate family, and they would tease her about me and make all kinds of remarks to tease her one way or another. None of them knew any of my family very well except her dad knew my dad because he purchased syrup from him. My stepmother wanted me to stay away from Mema and marry her niece from Autryville, but it never happened. However, I did date the other girl a few times with no good response. I then met Mema's extended family, and we all learned to love one another very much as they all saw a different person in me than Mema did at that time. It was especially true with Great-Great Grandma Matt Norman. She loved me from the start and defended me when Mema said anything derogatory about me. I had done something that Mema did not like at the time. She had told Grandma that "I would not marry him if he was the last man on earth." Grandma told her, "Virginia, that is the man you will marry." Obviously, she was correct in her assumption. I was a good-mannered and well-behaved young man and was not one to push myself on anyone. Her family received me extremely well, and every one of her uncles and aunts were at our wedding except the one that lived in Indian Town, Florida, Aunt Lucille Norman Stripling. While we were very much in love at that time, Mema was a senior in high school and needed to graduate before getting married. I joined the Navy in October 1951 and was gone for a long time but stayed in touch with Mema by writing to her. I went through the Navy boot camp; another Navy school in Jacksonville, Florida; and then was transferred to another Navy school in Memphis, Tennessee. After graduation from this school, I was transferred to a squadron at San Diego, California. After being there for several months, I was chosen to go on a deployment to the Panama Canal Zone in South America. While there I corresponded with Mema by writing her love letters almost every day. We seemed to bond very well, and it looked as if we were getting in deeper than either of us had thought possible being so far away. During this deployment, I asked Mema by mail if she would marry me, and things got out of hand from there on. Of course she accepted, and we started making plans to be married while I was home on leave after returning from the Canal Zone in early April of 1953. Mema and her family had made all the plans for the wedding as I was not here for any of the functions. I came home on leave from San Diego with some of my buddies who helped me drive my car from San Diego, California, in about three days. It was great a thrill to arrive home and see Mema after such a long time and after so many things had happened between us in the past few months. I had grown a beard and a goatee while in South America, and Mema did not like the looks of it very much. After meeting her for the first time in months and after our hugs and kisses were completed, Mema said to me, "That goatee has to go." By the time I picked her up at school that afternoon, it was gone. I should have known right then that she was going to be the boss of the family.

Things started happening real fast as we had to plan and execute our wedding and go on a honeymoon before I left to go back to San Diego. I just stood back as usual and let Mema do her thing, and everything went very well. First, Mema had to request and receive permission from the student counselor at Moultrie High School, Ms. Ethel Adams, in order that we could get married prior to her graduating. As this was the first time anyone had made such a request, Ms. Adams reluctantly granted Mema's request along with her heartfelt congratulations and best wishes for the future. She wished us a long and happy life together.

Second, I had to face this big ole rough-looking guy and ask his permission to marry his daughter. We had a long sort of pleasant discussion. After he had made me squirm for a while (I believe he did so reluctantly), he said that we had Mema's mother's and his blessings for us to be married. His only big request was that I treat his daughter with respect and be good to her. This was their main concern for both of their daughters. I assured him that I would always take care of Mema (it was Virginia at that time) and be good to her, and I have tried to fulfill my promise to Mema's parents and to our Lord the best I could. We had our blood test performed at the health department and then bought the marriage license with five dollars that I had borrowed from my dad. Everything went into place; and we were married on April 25, 1953, in our current home, which was Mema's parents. It was a very great wedding, and Mema was a very beautiful bride, as attested by the photos available from the occasion. It was supported very well by all her family and most especially by Aunt Rose, who came from Augusta, Georgia, along with her Jewish husband, Uncle Hyman Cohen. Of course she always wanted to run things and spread her wealth around to us poor Southern folks. Mema selected Aunt Edith to be her matron of honor and I selected Uncle Gene to be my best man. The house was full of our relatives and friends, and it was decorated exceptionally beautiful. The ceremony was performed by Mema's pastor, Brother McCorvey of Hopewell Baptist Church. Mom appeared to be very happy for us, and Dad was all tensed up over giving his daughter away to a sailor boy. Not knowing any more about me than he did, he was apprehensive of what he was doing. After all the pomp and show was over, Mema and I left to go on our honeymoon, which was in an apartment in Moultrie borrowed from my Aunt Pansy, my dad's sister. It was a very rainy night; and some relatives did not make the wedding because of the muddy, slick, and sloppy roads and bad weather. After a couple of days alone with me, Mema was ready to go back to her family's home so we could be with them until I had to return to the Navy.

We were hoping that this would be something good, and as far as I know, it has been a marriage of bliss. And the rest is history. I could not have married a better person to spend my life with than Mama. She has always been so supportive of me and my endeavors, whatever they were. Now I must admit that she has corrected my course several times, but it was always in a good and loving constructive way.

SOMETIMES BAD THINGS HAPPEN TO GOOD PEOPLE

DENVER TO ORLANDO EPISODE

Upon arriving at Orlando Florida International Airport from Denver, Colorado, after visiting my brother and his wife (Gene and Mary) for a week and after an ordeal at the baggage claim area, Betty, Pat, and I retrieved my truck from the long-term parking facility. Since meals are no longer served on a normal flight, we thought we would stop at Cracker Barrel and have dinner on the way out to Orange Park, Florida. We had no incidents after getting into the truck nor any on the way to the restaurant. Subsequent to finishing our meal, we proceeded to depart for our destination by getting situated in our truck. I started the truck and backed out of the parking space as I always do; however, I noticed that my brake pedal went all the way to the floor and the truck would not stop as it normally did. I desperately maneuvered the truck back into the parking space and evaluated the problem the best I could. I had very little brake fluid in the master cylinder and told that to Pat. He walked over to a service station and purchased a can of brake fluid, which I poured into the master cylinder. I attempted to check the brakes once more, and they did no better than previously. Further evaluation did not indicate any fluid leakage at the brake drums or hydraulic lines.

Since we were unable to drive the truck, we proceeded to hunt a motel in which to spend the night. Cracker Barrel was about to close, so I had to get some numbers from them as soon as possible; but it didn't help at all. We had three cell phones, and each of us was calling different motels trying to find accommodations.

We also needed a rental car, and the airport was a long way from our current location. I walked over to the rental business where I had parked my truck before flying to Denver. I asked the agent at the desk if I could ride his shuttle to the airport to rent an automobile, and he agreed. After arriving at the airport, I went to the agency that I had called and reserved an automobile. The only card I had was a credit card, and they only accepted debit cards; therefore, I was out of luck. I went to the next auto rental and attempted to rent an automobile from them, and their rules were the same as the last agency; so no luck there either. During this time, I had walked to the third floor of the airport since there were no agents on duty at the agency from which I thought I had rented the first automobile. I was getting very tired by this time as I had walked a long way trying to find a car rental with no success. This agent told me that there was an agency on the third floor of the next building that would accept a credit card. I walked back up to the third floor to find this agency, and it was not easy. I walked and walked until I finally found the agency, and I rented an automobile from them. Finally, I was on my way back to where Betty and Pat were attempting to locate a motel. They had been calling since I left and had finally found one across town in Saint Cloud. We loaded the luggage into the rental car and took off to our home away from home. By this time, we had been up about twenty hours and were very tired. We arrived there about 2:30 AM and asked for a wake-up call at 6:30 AM so we could return to my truck and locate a Ford agency at which I could have my truck repaired. We arrived back at the Cracker Barrel to find everything as we left it the night before. First things first, we went into the restaurant and ate breakfast.

Once back outside, Pat located a towing facility, and this gentleman towed us to Tropical Ford on the Orange Blossom Trail. I immediately registered my truck, and they eventually diagnosed my problem as a failed brake booster pump of which none was in stock at that facility. Once they ordered the booster, it took the agency about two hours to receive it from the warehouse. By this time, I was getting frustrated with this situation, and I let the service manager know my concerns about the lack of urgency in my situation and our need to get back to Orange Park. He nodded his head as if he understood, but his sympathy was not very visible.

In order to expedite our return trip, I asked the manager if he could take me to the rental agency to return my car. He analyzed the location of the airport and informed me that it was a couple of blocks out of their facilities jurisdiction; therefore, he would not take us to the car rental agency. Time was dragging on, and it seemed that they would never have my truck repaired today. I kept pressing them to get it ready. Finally, at about 5:30 PM, they drove my truck to the front for checkout. There was some confusion about the extent of my repair policy, so we had another discussion with the agency and the insurance company. Finally, we came to terms about the amount I was liable for and checked out ASAP.

Now that all the fun was over, we still had to return our rental, and it was a long distance from the Ford dealership. We obtained directions from a guy that had lived in Orlando all his life, and he thought that we should understand all the roads he named for us to arrive at the rental agency. By trial and error, we finally arrived at the rental agency; however, only rental automobiles could go to the third floor, so Betty and Pat had to wait until I checked my vehicle back in and walk—yes, walk—back to the waiting area to where my truck was parked. I eased back into the traffic and guided myself through this maze until I had some easier driving as the traffic was lighter than around the airport. We found our direction back to I-4 and sped north as fast as possible. We drove for about thirty minutes until we saw a restaurant that we all recognized, and we stopped there for dinner.

After about an hour at this place, we proceeded north to Orange Park at a reasonable pace. Finally, we arrived back in Orange Park, and each of us settled into our own little abode for a safe night's sleep: Pat at his home on Hopkins Street and Aunt Betty and I went to Aunt Lynn's.

One can read this epistle and not seem to be very concerned about the total situation; however, they would have to walk the distance I did being an old man and enduring each phase of the total episode to understand the gravity of our situation and the endurance it took to accomplish the total episode of the situation. Hopefully, I will never need to experience this situation again and, hopefully, neither will any of my family. It is frustrating when it appears that the agencies out there to serve us do it haphazardly or with the least amount of zeal and enthusiasm. Automobile dealerships should initiate the same process as in the hospitals. Evaluate the situation and assign a priority to it and treat it as a triage in the hospital. I am not asking for sympathy in my situation but am only illustrating how things may go wrong in most any situation, and it appears that we have no control over our destiny in most situations. I have to admit that I did do a lot of praying as I was going from place to place because there are some treacherous areas within the confines of an airport and automobile rental spaces. Be careful in any of these places, and be on the lookout for the danger spots as they lurk in all areas of transportation facilities.

My Military Career

DEDICATION

I would like to dedicate this part of my book to a wonderful and loyal friend—my wife, Virginia Norman Eldridge—and also to my children, Larry and Lynn Eldridge. My wife kept everything going at home while I was away so many times and kept my uniforms in great shape for me to attend my drills whenever scheduled. She spent so many days alone and not knowing if I would make it home or not while flying my missions both in the daytime and night flights. It was always a pleasure to return home to my family no matter what circumstances I had gone through while on Naval reserve duty. There were so many things that I could have done with my children during their maturing years, but I was absent from duty serving in the Naval reserves. We missed out on so much, and I ask that they forgive me for that time away and understand that it means much more to Mema and I now than we ever dreamed it would. I enjoyed my time in the Navy, Naval reserves, and the Air Force reserves very much, and it made me proud to represent America while in the foreign countries.

Last but by far the least, I want to thank my Lord for allowing me to perform my duties throughout my military career without loss of limb or life. He has taken me through many parlous situations with no notable harm or injury. Being in aviation, one never knows what may happen at any given moment. The Lord knows that I have had some exciting situations; however, I was protected by my God to return safely to my family.

God bless America.

MILITARY CAREER

One day I decided that I was tired of picking cotton and working at the local Air Force base as an airplane mechanic. I discussed this with some of my buddies, and we decided to join the Navy and see the world. We went to the local Navy recruiter's office to join, but he was not there. Three of the guys that were with me did not want to go to Valdosta to the Navy recruiter; therefore, they joined the Air Force in Moultrie. Buddy Walden, Floyd Wilder, and I went to Valdosta and joined the Navy. We went through a lot of preliminary testing and evaluations; and then we were sent to Jacksonville, Florida, for all the final induction processes. Once we had all our physical examinations, we were sworn into the United States Navy on October 4, 1951.

The physical examinations were a sight to behold as there were hundreds of boys going through one phase or another of the examination in several large rooms. In some of these rooms, we had on our shorts (to those of us that wore shorts), and in other rooms, we were as naked as the day we came into this world. Now that was a sight to behold as I had never seen that many naked men in my life. It appeared that the Navy corpsmen and doctors were making a game out of all the new boys from the country, and they would make jokes at us throughout the examination. After all the shots, poking, and body parts examinations, they finally told all of us to get dressed and report to a certain area for further information and certification. After dinner, they took us to a local hotel and checked us in for the night.

The next morning, we were taken to the train station and loaded on a special train for all the recruits that had been qualified for military duty. Each of us had our own bed set up and a special boxcar had been set up as a chow hall. This boxcar had a table down the middle, and it was braced so it wouldn't fall. We were served our meals on a regular military plastic tray, and we had to stand around the table to eat our meals. It was a treat to say the least, and we had to mind on our p's and q's to be able to eat while the train was traveling at high rates of speed. Most of the day was spent just looking out the window at the beautiful scenery or playing cards. At times our train would be directed to a side rail to wait on another train with higher priorities. There was no set time for us to wait, and they would let us off the train to roam around and scout the local area. On a couple of these occasions, some local girls would be curious about us being there and come to check us out. Of course, we would flirt with them, and maybe some addresses were exchanged for further use.

We finally made our way to San Diego, California, and were taken to the boot camp where we would remain for several weeks without any outside world contact with anyone. One of the first items on the agenda was issuing us an M1 rifle that we called a piece. We would learn how to disassemble, clean, and reassemble this gun to make it function as it should. You were to keep this piece with you at all times and never abuse it in any way. If you were caught abusing this piece, you would sleep with it. This was your source of survival, if need be. We would spend our time on the marching field, in the classroom, and actually participating in work concerning the welfare and safety of all sailors, such as fire drills and fire control. We would spend a lot of time in the water learning how to survive jumping off a sinking ship and how to elude fires that may be on the water due to fuel leaking from the ship. We were taught the correct procedures for jumping off a damaged ship in the middle of the ocean and the art of surviving with the clothes we wore. These procedures would enable sailors to remain in the water for a long time without much effort and make it safer for all concerned. Following these procedures would enhance our chance of survival and make it better for rescue personnel.

On the marching field, we learned many kinds of maneuvers in coordination with one another to enable our complete platoon to march in sequence and in step with one another. I did pretty good on the marching field and was soon selected to be one of the honor guards that carried the American and Navy flag. On each side of the flags there was a guard carrying a gun to protect our flags from other intruders. This was an honor position, and I enjoyed this very much.

After we had been there for about six weeks, we were taken to a location in the desert to learn about the rifle and its purpose. We would keep our rifle, which was called a piece, with us at all times as it was our only means for survival in an isolated place. We had to keep our piece cleaned at all times, and if you did not, the instructor would make you sleep with it until you had it cleaned and you could operate it carefully and safely without endangering anyone else.

I joined in October; therefore, I would be in San Diego during the month of December, and the word was that we would not be able to go home until we graduated from boot camp.

Since I had never been away from home on Christmas, I was very upset that I would not be with my brothers, sister, and other family members. Christmas had always been a joyful time for our family even though we did not get that much some years; however, we were together, and that was all that mattered to us.

However, someone gave us permission to go home on leave for Christmas, and we were very excited. We boarded a Greyhound bus and did not tarry too long in getting home. Each bus driver drove a specified time and to a certain town, then he was relieved by another one that drove us to the end of his route. We came from San Diego to Moultrie in about two-and-a-half days. These guys drove wide-open all the way as they knew we wanted to get home to our families. They would let some of the guys off along the way and keep on trucking to our most Southern point.

I had a great time while on leave and had a joyous Christmas with my family and friends. The time always passes fast when you are busy and when you are having a great time with all your friends and family. Of course, I had to tell all of them some "war" stories about my first two months in the Navy, and it intrigued most of them as they had never traveled outside of Colquitt County; however, here ole Buddy was already a seasoned traveler. While gone since October, Dad had bought a Buick Century car that was very nice and drove like a dream. He let me use it a lot while home as I had many things to do and places to go. It was soon time for me to catch the bus back to San Diego, which I did reluctantly; however, if I had chosen not to go back, the Navy would come and get me for being absent from duty without authority. And then they would put me in the brig, or the Navy jail. I arrived back in San Diego and resumed my training until I graduated from boot camp in January of 1952. I was very blessed to graduate in the top 10 percent of my class. Since I graduated so high in my class, I was able to choose a school for additional training in my naval career. I was proud for myself but saddened for my two buddies that I had joined with as they were assigned to an aircraft carrier in the Pacific Ocean. I was transferred to A&E Preparatory School in Jacksonville, Florida. This was an eight-week school, and it prepared me for many aircraft maintenance positions that I could apply for when I graduated in March of 1952. Jacksonville Naval Air Station was only about 160 miles from Moultrie, and that enabled me to come home to see all my family and friends more often.

During my training at this school, I studied more about aircraft and aircraft components. My grades at this school would determine the actual field of aircraft maintenance that I was most adapted to. During my time at this school, I would come home on weekends, and sometimes, I would see Mema and her family for periods of time. It was always good to see Mema as she was such a pretty green-eyed brunette, and sometimes she would let me steal a kiss or two before I left to go back to school. I would carry this memory with me until I returned home again. On one of these weekend trips home, I went with Mema to a function at her old elementary school. We saw many of our friends and relatives there and had a great time. Of course, I was in my Navy uniform, and that was an attraction for many of our friends as they had not seen me in many months.

This is a preface to what I am going to relate to you so you will understand how embarrassed I was at that moment of contact. In the military, you are supposed to salute an officer with your right hand upon approaching them; however, when Mema and were going to our automobile, I turned the corner of the old school house and was face-to-face with a Naval officer. Since I had my right arm around Mema's waist, all I could do was salute him with my left hand. This was awkward but legal in some circumstances, of which I was in one of those. He saluted me and gave me big grin of approval as we passed each other.

After graduating from this school, I was transferred to an AD (A) School in Memphis, Tennessee. During my final evaluations, the Navy determined that due to my test scores and my previous experience as an aircraft engine worker, my best field of expertise would be in the aircraft engine profession. This was a more advanced school, and they taught me many facets of maintenance on the Navy's aircraft engines. The Navy's aircraft had many functions, and each had an engine that would make its mission better. Some of our aircraft were fighters, some were training planes, and some were bombers. Each had a specific mission to accomplish during the time of war. During peace time, the aircrews mostly trained to make themselves better qualified in case there was a war or an emergency. I was trained to start and run the engines on the various aircraft we had in our training phase. We were trained to work on the engines to make them perform better, and we were trained to do periodic maintenance on all the engines as well. Periodic maintenance is required to keep the aircraft ready for flying whenever needed for any purpose or occasion. During this time, we were also trained in other Navy functions such as firefighting, swimming, classes in math, science, and a lot of Navy customs and traditions. It was imperative that we were able to escape from a burning aircraft or a burning ship in a quick and safe manner.

This is a short story about this duty station. While in the school at Jacksonville, I met a sailor by the name of Larry Compagna. His family owned an auto body shop and lived in a very nice neighborhood in Memphis, Tennessee. He could not go to Memphis for the other school, so he gave me his parents' name, address, and telephone number. His mother was a volunteer at the Naval hospital at Millington Naval Base. I called them one day and introduced myself over the phone. They asked me to visit them, and that was a very welcomed invitation at any time. I made arrangements to meet them, and they took me to their home. It was such a blessing to have someone such as them to visit with while I was off duty at the school. When I arrived at their home, Mom Compagna showed me to "my" room, which, by the way, was Larry's room when he was there. She had some civilian clothes laid out on the bed for me, and they fit perfect as I was the same size as Larry. They had another son younger than Larry, and he made me feel right at home as well. Since they were Catholic, they made arrangements for a friend of theirs to take me to his Baptist church each Sunday morning that I was there.

These were extremely nice folks, and I have never felt any more at home than I did when I was there. I continued to visit them until July 1952 when I graduated from the AD (A) school. I remained in contact with them for several years; and when I was discharged from the Navy in September 1955, Mema, Larry and I went by to see them in Memphis, Tennessee. They were so thrilled to see me and my family as I was equally as glad to see them and for them to meet my family as well. When Lynn was stationed at Millington Naval Base in Memphis in 2002, I made arrangements to meet Larry and his wife, Ann, for dinner in Cordova, near Lynn's apartment. It was such a good reunion, and we e-mailed each other from time to time. It is so good to have friends such as this family was and continued to be until each of their deaths. He, his wife, and both of his parents are gone now; but our memory still lives on for the many wonderful things that they did for me while I was a stranger from nowhere. God will provide you happiness and joy even in some of your darkest times, and you can count on that. End of short story.

Subsequent to graduating from the school in Memphis, I went on leave again in Moultrie and had another great time with my family and friends, especially Mema. While on leave, I purchased my first car, which was a light-green two-door 1950 Ford. I thought I was king stuff and had the world by the tail. I spent a lot of time with Mema and her family during my leave and got to know them very well. They all seemed to like me or at least they tolerated me to a certain degree just to satisfy Mema. As usual, my leave went too fast, and I had to leave Mema and go to Miramar Naval Base, which was near San Diego, California.

I left home to drive to San Diego, California, by myself. I had never driven very far before and did not know what was in store for me as the trip unfolded through the states that I had to drive through. As I remember, it was not all that boring since I had a good radio to listen to, and it would keep me awake. I would drive as long as I could and then pull over for a night's sleep; however, I cannot remember where I spent all my nights except my third night. I had driven through Texas all day and arrived in El Paso, Texas, around dusk dark. I found a USO open and pulled into the parking lot to investigate the possibility of staying there overnight. It was okay, and I stayed there that night. I mentioned my destination to someone, and the word was received by this one young sailor who was spending the night there also. He asked if I would drop him off in Los Angles, California, for a certain amount of money. I looked at my planned route and the new route to determine if I could do this guy a favor. I decided that I could, and we took off for Los Angles. We made the trip okay, and then I went on south to Miramar Naval Air Station, which was only about 120 miles.

Miramar was the master jet base of the West Coast and had many different types of aircraft in several squadrons stationed aboard the base. I happened to be assigned to a photographic squadron, which had the Navy's PB4Y bombers as their primary aircraft to accomplish their tasks for the Navy. This was a large four-engine aircraft that was previously used by the Air Force as a bomber (B-24 Liberator) in World War II (photo on the next page). I was taught how to perform maintenance on the engines and the associated parts to keep them in good running condition. I had not been there long before my chief realized that I worked well and was proficient in my work. He assigned me to a night-shift duty, and it was easier for me.

We had other duties to perform while in the squadron, such as guard duty on the flight line where our aircraft were parked. It was our duty to keep all unauthorized personnel away from the aircraft as we did not want any sabotage done to them. Our watch time was normally a four-hour shift either in the barracks or on the flight line. This time was a nonduty period of time that all personnel had to perform. We were also responsible for keeping our sleeping area of the barracks clean and in an orderly condition. We washed our own clothes and had to keep them clean at all times. Each morning our sleeping quarters were inspected and the clothes that we wore were as well. We had to be clean and neat at all times.

During my course of working in the squadron, I was able to mix with many of the other personnel assigned there and learn a little about their job and what their function was relating to the operation of the squadron. We had a large room set aside for our breaks and leisure times, and it was called a coffee mess. This is a place where many of us hung out when we were between jobs on aircraft or where we ate our lunch. They sold various items to eat and drink, but it was mostly a coffee break room. It was also an area where many of the sailors told a lot of things that were hard to believe, and some of them you wouldn't believe. We had sailors from many different states within the United States, and they each had a different way of expressing themselves and a different speaking dialogue and mannerism. I soon began to mix with many of them and soon became good friends that went on liberty together in Mexico and in the surrounding towns and beaches. Some of the guys were married, and I was invited to their homes for dinner or just to hang out for a short time on weekends.

Our base was not too far from Tijuana, Mexico, and during liberty some of us would go over to the Mexican side and shop or just hang out for a different atmosphere. It is now one of the most notorious places for drugs and murders in Mexico. The gangs are terrible, and most Americans do not even go to this place anymore. Mema and I spent many hours just walking around the town and shopping or eating the Mexican food, which was very good. We were walking hand in hand one afternoon, and this Mexican came up to us and asked us, "Do you want to get married?" I told him that we were already married, and without batting an eye, he asked me, "Do you want to get divorced?"

I replied, "No, sir, we do not."

I kept writing Mema and telling her most of the stuff I was doing and how things were going in the squadron and with some of my particular friends. She would keep me posted on all the news in and around Moultrie, which was not very exciting to me. Some of the people Mema knew at school were friends of mine also, and they would keep me posted on her and some of her activities in school and out of school. Some of my friends would tell me that if Mema did not receive a letter from me, her mood would change and she would seem a little depressed. I never knew how my letters would affect someone so much because my penmanship was terrible and I never had that much to write about. I guess it was the psychological effect on her more than the content of the letter.

I was only an airman at the time and was being trained in the squadron; however, I learned my job very fast and was noted for doing a good job and doing it correctly. My chiefs spotted my ability to do a good job and recommended me as a flight crew member of one of the PB4Ys. I was indoctrinated on the operations of the aircraft and the functions of all the systems so I could assist the plane captain in conducting preflights, postflights, and servicing of the aircraft. Preflighting the aircraft was a procedure where you would check all the moving parts of the aircraft and make sure that there was adequate oil, gasoline, water, and other survival equipment on the aircraft. Our crew would run the engines of the aircraft to ensure that they were operating correctly and within the established perimeters set by the manufacturer.

My duty as a second mechanic was to fly in the rear of the aircraft and watch for other aircraft and keep an eye on the four engines as we flew. Just watching the engines would assist in detecting any oil leaks or any other malfunctions if they arose. My careful observation of the engines operating would be useful in the event something did happen to warrant the repair of any of our engines.

It was about this time that I met one of the best friends that I have ever had. Jim and Earlene Swanson proved to be an extraordinary couple that would remain in our lives for as long as they lived or were functional. Jim came in the coffee mess one day looking for someone to stand his duty for the weekend, Friday night until Sunday afternoon. He wanted to be with his wife when their daughter, Debra, was born. I told him I would stand his duty if he would like for me to, then he inquired about how much it would cost. I told him that I would not charge him anything if that was a legitimate claim. At that time, I could get twenty dollars for standing weekend duty for someone, and that was a lot of money in 1952. I was only making ninety-eight dollars a month at that time. He was the proudest person in the building as nobody else would stand his duty and he thought he would miss the birth of his daughter.

After his daughter was born and everything was back to normal at home, he and his wife invited me to dinner one night and wanted me to spend the weekend with them at their home in Escondido, California. They lived in a small home on her parent's farm very near to the parents. I became acquainted very quickly with Earlene's family, the Zickafooses, and loved them very much over the years. They were just plain ole folks and took me in as another "son" while I stayed with them on the weekends. Dad Zickafoose wore overalls just like Mema's dad did and grew a lot of hay and vegetables on his farm. As time went on, I would babysit Debra and ride her around in my car to keep her satisfied until she went to sleep, then I would bring her back home to her parents.

Months turned into years, and after Debra had a son, she nick named him Budric after me. That is one of the best compliments that I have ever had in my life from another family. That little boy had a birth name of Eric and is a senior in college in 2010. We have kept in touch with the Swansons since 1952 and have visited them on several occasions in the past fifty-seven years, and the last time was when I helped do his eulogy in May of 2007. I lost a dear friend that I will always remember. After the funeral, Earlene gave me Jim's model of the aircraft we flew in, the PB4Y. Thanksgiving and Christmas of 1952 came and went, and we had to plan on a deployment to South America for about three months. This deployment was to leave in early January of 1953, and our home away from home was to be France Field in Coco Solo, Canal Zone. We did leave in early January of 1953 and flew into our new home in Navy transport aircraft. Jim

Swanson went with me on this deployment; and we worked, played, and partied together. We soon unpacked all our equipment and set up shop for our normal maintenance procedures on our squadron aircraft, the PB4Y. We soon got acclimated to the weather and hours of operation, which were different from Alaska. We were in the tropical zone and had to dress accordingly for work and for play. We had a lot of leisure time to do what we wanted to, including going on liberty together in Coco Solo, which consisted of all-black natives. The buildings in this town had steel bars installed between them to keep the natives from taking sailors into the alley and robbing them. It was a rough town, and we did not go there at night due to the serious nature of the risks involved. Jim and I spent a lot of time writing to our family, and I wrote Mema every day I was there. Some of the letters were not very long, but they were mushy with love and sweetness to her. During this time away from Mema, I had asked her to marry me if she would, and she had accepted. I told you the letters were mushy. I believe that the Lord meant for us to be together as He arranged our letters in the correct perspective for both of us. I was looking forward to getting home and accomplishing my main goal of all the letter writing: getting married. Jim and I also spent a lot of time exercising and working out in the gym to keep our waist slim and our body toned. We also swam a lot in the local pool near our barracks, and our tan was great.

We shared the aircraft hangar with an amphibian aircraft squadron that did search and rescue. Their aircraft had removable wheels that had to be reattached when they landed in the water and before the aircraft were beached or could come ashore. This was difficult task and could only be accomplished by white sailors due to barracuda being in the water. They had several black sailors attacked due to the white part of the bottom of their feet flashing while in the water. The fish were attracted to this flash, and the sailors had to be removed from the task of installing wheels on the aircraft after landing. While in this area, Jim and I wanted to go through the Panama Canal Zone locks just for the experience. We boarded a small Navy ship and did just that. As soon as we were through the first locks, we had to wait in Lake Gatoon for about six hours before we could go through the lowering locks on the other side of the lake. This is the only process in the world like this. The ships are raised in the locks on the Pacific Ocean side and lowered on the Atlantic Ocean side due to the difference in the height in the water levels. Doesn't it look like God would have made both sides the same level, or did he do this for a specific purpose? Who knows? Once we arrived in the city of Panama, we boarded a bus to take us back to the base. We had had a long day on the water. This made me glad that I was in the Naval Aviation instead of on the ships. The Lord blessed me in keeping me in a safe place.

Some of us wanted to go out in the jungle and spend the night and camp out. We received all the rations from the galley and prepared for the trip. After arriving in the dense woods, we gathered wood and started a fire. We were told that the big cats would not come around if you had a fire burning. We ate dinner around the fire and told wild stories about a lot of things, and then it was time to go to sleep. We had made us a place in the trees to sleep and stoked the fire with plenty of wood before retiring for the night. During the night, we heard all types of noises and hardly slept due the uncertainty of what was watching us. At daybreak we ate breakfast and sort of broke camp and headed back to the base. It was a good experience, but I do not believe that I would do again. Soon our deployment was over, and we went back to our base at Miramar. We soon had our deployment gear off-loaded and back in its normal place. It was good to be back at Miramar where our friends and some of the crew's family were. It is always a glorious reunion when we come off deployment even if the deployment is only for a short time. Several of us from South Georgia had applied for leave to go home as soon as we were back at Miramar. I was going home to marry Mema, the love of my life, on April 25, 1953. There were four of us going home together, and only three of us would swap driving.

It was a good trip, and we made it in two-and-one-half days as we only stopped for food and fuel. We let one of the guys off in Albany, Georgia, and one off in Doerun, Georgia: David Chapman. I did not know until recent years that David married Dick Traylor's daughter. Dick owned the Moultrie Tire and Recapping Company in

Moultrie. Her brother, Rodney, told me a few years ago that David was a heavy drinker and had died only a few months prior to me learning that he was living in Doerun, Georgia. He also attended our wedding as a special friend.

Just a short story on David Chapman: David was a friend of mine from Doerun, Georgia. He was a mechanic in our squadron and was a very likable person; however, he could not handle alcohol of any portion. David would do the strangest and dumbest things when drunk and not remember any of them.

While in South America, David got drunk one night and came to work the next morning the same way. He got up on an engine stand under one of our engines and tied his hands up in the air so to look like he was working. A chief from another squadron watched him for a while and then went to our chief to report that "that sailor has not moved in fifteen minutes as I was watching him." Our chief went to the stand and found David tied up as if he was working and sound asleep. He dismissed him immediately and sent him to the barracks. This was David at some of his tricks.

Another incident was when he was being discharged. David walked around the squadron with the base of his shoe was flapping as he walked. His shoe was worn out, but he was not going to buy anymore Navy shoes since he was being discharged that day. I did not hear from David anymore and had not heard where he was until I heard someone mention a David Chapman at the Moultrie Tire Store that Rodney co-owned with his brother. By then it was too late for me to go see David. End of David's story.

After arriving home, the first place I went was to see my soon-to-be bride. We had our greetings and salutations over in a short while, and then we began to talk about each other's looks and so forth. I had grown a beard and a goatee while on deployment, and I thought it looked good. However, Mema told me that it had to go. You see, she was demanding even back then. That afternoon when I drove to school to get my sweetheart, my beard and goatee were gone. She liked my face much better without that stuff, and I had to agree that it did not do much for me. We soon started making plans for our wedding by getting our blood test and talking to Mema's preacher, Brother McCorvey of Hopewell Baptist Church. We had our blood test done, and then I went and purchased our marriage license from the courthouse and was ready to go as for my part of the ceremony.

Mema had made all the arrangements and did everything just right for our wedding. She was granted permission by the school to get married by our student counselor, Ms. Ethel Adams. We had plenty of friends and relatives there to witness our ceremony. Aunt Edith was Mema's maid of honor and Uncle Gene was my best man. After the ceremony and the reception, we left to go on our honeymoon, which was in an apartment loaned to us by my Aunt Pansy, my dad's sister. We only stayed there a night or two, and then we went back to Mema's home for the remainder of my time home. We had a great time as all of Mema's family was there except Aunt Lucille.

Mema was a senior in high school and had to stay in Moultrie to graduate, and I was getting ready for a deployment to Alaska. My buddies and I drove back to Miramar, and it was an uneventful trip as we did real good going back. After arriving back at Miramar, we started preparing for our deployment to Kodiak, Alaska, in May of 1953. We flew to Alaska in a Navy transport and arrived at our new home safe and sound. This place was different from any other place that I had ever been. There was volcanic ash all over the place and hardly anything would grow there. We set up shop in our hangar and began working on the aircraft as they flew in from the United States. Many of them had oil leak problems, and they had to be repaired prior to another flight. We did more than just work on aircraft in Alaska. We went fishing in the bay and in rivers and caught salmon and the large fish halibut. While at the Russian river one day, one of my friends was fishing on the opposite side of us. He was not aware that there was a large female grizzly bear near him obstructed by trees and bushes. We warned him of his danger, and he hastily retreated back to our side. Unbeknownst to him, he was fishing between the mother and her cubs, which is a no-no in the woods. These mother bears protected their cubs from all predators and other wild animals with much diligence.

I worked in the mess hall (dining room to civilians) preparing salads while on KP. Some others did the cooking and getting the food ready for serving to all the military personnel stationed on the island. We had to scrub the floors after each meal so everything was clean and sanitary. We had plenty to eat and drink and made sure that there were plenty of desserts available for all personnel. Since we were so near the rotation of the sun to the earth, our nights would be very short at times, and there would even be daylight at eleven o'clock at night. We could see well enough at that time of night to work on our aircraft without lights. It was so weird that we needed blinds in the barracks windows to keep the sunlight out at night or else we could not sleep. Since there was no place to go on liberty, we would spend much of our spare time playing cards or exercising. Of course, I would spend some of my spare time writing Mema to let her know what I was doing and what was going on in my life on the island. It was always good to receive letters from Mema and my family while being so far away from home. You have to remember that we did not have the luxury of telephones over there, and cell phones were not even a dream at that time. When you were away from home in those days, you did not hear or see anyone for months.

While walking to the hangar one day, I heard someone call my name from a distance. I turned to see a buddy of mine from boot camp that I had not seen since we graduated. He asked me, "Were you from Moultrie, Georgia?" and I answered in the affirmative or yes. He told me that a sailor from Moultrie was stationed in Kodiak in the electronic building just across the grinder. We called this guy, and it turned out to be a classmate of mine, Ronald Tucker, whom I had not seen since graduating in 1951. Ronald and I talked for a long time and said our goodbyes at that time. I never saw Ronald again as I was leaving Alaska to return to Miramar. However, in 2001, we met again in Moultrie as we were on the class reunion planning committee together. It was good to see him again, and we remained in contact on the planning committee until he passed away in September 2007.

In September of 1953, we returned to Miramar Naval Station and resumed duties as we were before deployment. Going back to work on all the local aircraft and doing our normal duties, such as standing watch and going on liberty with some of our old friends that we had not seen in a long time. While in Alaska, I left my car parked at Jim Swanson's home so he could keep the battery charged by running it from time to time. I came out to their home often, and we really enjoyed our friendship very much. We had received some new AJ-2P aircraft while I was deployed to Alaska. These new aircraft were designed for carrying the atomic bomb; however, there was a delay in manufacture, and it missed its mission. This aircraft had two R-3350 reciprocating engines and one J33 jet engine. This was one of the first aircraft with a mixed engine assigned to our squadron and, I believe, the first ones in the Navy. We trained on this aircraft's maintenance and systems by working on them and in the classroom. It was a much more sophisticated aircraft than the old PB4Y and more difficult to perform maintenance on. It had a crew of four instead a crew of ten as the PB4Y did and was a much faster aircraft.

As soon as I returned from Alaska, I notified Mema, who was staying with her parents in Georgia. Of course, she was excited that I was back at Miramar safe and sound and doing well. She advised me that she was coming out to California and for me to be ready. I was ready for her to come; in fact, Jim, Earlene, and I had already chosen an apartment and were just waiting on Mema. Jim and Earlene went with me to the train station to get Mema upon arrival. They were happy to finally meet Mema, and they gave her a great welcome. Jim thought she was a beautiful girl, and I agreed with him wholeheartedly. She was the prettiest thing in the train terminal, and I was so proud for her to arrive safely into my arms.

Mema and I went to our apartment as she was very tired and we really wanted to be alone, which was the first time since we were married in April. We only lived in this apartment for a short time because Mema did not like it. The landlord let us move to the one downstairs, which was not much different. After staying there a month or so, we moved to an apartment owned by the same people, and it was behind their house. We were anxious for Mema to get pregnant so we could have our own baby, but it did not happen for some time. The lady we rented from told us not to give up because every woman that had lived there ended up pregnant. We were disappointed each month when she was not pregnant. One month she thought she was pregnant, and we were over at Jim and Earlene's when Earlene told me that Mema was very upset; so I went to console her best that I could. Lo and behold, our landlady was right! Mema got pregnant in November of 1953. The apartment was furnished with a gas stove and a gas refrigerator, but that did not work out for Mema as it made her very sick. We hated to leave our landlord, but we moved to the base housing so Mema would not be sick all the time. We lived in a mobile home that was only eight feet wide and twenty-seven feet long. It was very close, and we could not even pass in the hallway, but we were happy just to be with each other and to have Mema pregnant. We would play cards from time to time, and Mema was not very good at that. She would get very frustrated when she lost and would sling the cards all over the floor. That was a new game, and I called it "Fifty-two card pick up." We did have a great time together and enjoyed being alone and doing whatever we wanted. Mema would crave some things, and I would go get it for her on occasions. Once she was craving shrimp or something, and I had to drive about twenty miles to the beach to purchase them. That was all part of the situation at hand. It was a trying time for us as most anything would make Mema sick to her stomach, and I had to give way when she made that unusual sound that let me know she was coming to the bathroom. I would have to do the grocery shopping because coffee was at the front of the commissary. That would make Mema sick, and she would have to run out to the car and wait for me. Whenever possible, we would go to see Jim and Earlene on the weekend and have a great visit.

However, in January of 1954, Jim was chosen to go back on deployment to South America and, this time, without me to be his best sidekick. On January 6, the flight crews left our squadron area for their flight to France Field in Coco Solo, Canal Zone. One of the aircraft crashed on landing, and seven of my friends died in the crash and shortly thereafter. Five men died in the crash, one died on the way to the hospital, and one died the next day; however, the best miracle of all was that seven men survived this terrible crash. Most of the survivors were injured very severely, but all recovered within time. Some of them had multiple surgeries but lived to tell of that horrible day in Coco Solo. I have met with one of the survivors on several occasions, and he relives this accident whenever he talks about it. Jim Swanson was one of the first sailors to the crash, and he told me that it was very bad. He assisted one of our friends to safety, but he died later that night in the hospital from multiple burns over most of his body. I was very close to several of the ones that died and had been on a deployment in Alaska with them the prior year. They brought some of the bodies back to San Diego; and I went to the funeral of Pappy Fry, an older first class who was extremely good to me and all the others he knew. He was one of the most-liked ones in our squadron at that time. Some pictures and articles describing the crash are attached for your interest. Out of respect for my fellow shipmates, I will list the names of each person on board the fatal aircraft.

The dead are Lieutenant jg Everett Griffin, Chief Raymond Pavesich, AD1 Clarence "Pappy" Fry (plane captain), PH3 Charles Kratt, PH3 Harold Lane, and A03 Robert Parmenter Jr. (This guy was a very close friend of mine, and during our deployment to Alaska he called me Horomie. He left Alaska early due his wife's sickness and had to go on this deployment to qualify for separation bonus at discharge), and Arthur Manor, one of our cooks for the deployment at the chow hall. He was the only black sailor on the plane. He was on deployment with me in January of 1953 and was returning to Coco Solo to marry his sweetheart from the previous deployment.

The injured are Lieutenant jg John Toohey, Lieutenant jg Robert Bixler, AM2 Andrew Hinkle, AD1 David Ross, AD2 Robert Delk, AD2 Kenneth Kliewer (this is the one that Mema and I have had several reunions within the past few years), and TR3 Clarence Schneider. As far as I know, all these men recovered to a reasonable healthy lifestyle.

This photo is a picture of the aircraft that crashed in the Canal Zone and also the aircraft type that I flew in as an aircrew member in California, the Canal Zone, and Alaska.

We were scheduled to go to Alaska on another deployment in June of 1954, so we had to make preparations to get Mema back to Georgia so our baby, Larry, would be born in Georgia. Not only did we not like that idea of Larry being born in California, but Mema would be by herself in a strange place and in a strange land. I submitted for leave to drive Mema home so she could be with her mother and in a familiar surrounding when Larry was born. We bought a small trailer and packed all our belongings and started toward Moultrie, Georgia. One of my sailor friends and his wife were riding with us as far as his home in middle Texas. They were Tom and Rosie Patten, and she was about five months pregnant as Mema was. Tom and I switched driving just to make it easier for one another. Everything went very good until we were between Midland and Odessa, Texas. There we ran into some unmarked road construction. I had driven all night, and it was early Sunday morning just before daybreak that I snagged a large hole in the road with one of my trailer wheels. The impact caused me to overcorrect, and I got hung up on the edge of the rough pavement and flipped our car. The car flipped one time and spun out of control and landed on its wheels facing the way from which we were coming. After all the excitement was over and we all crawled out of the car, we discovered that nobody was hurt and everything was okay except our small bird, which was killed. The back window was busted out, and the car was totaled; however, the Lord had blessed us to be in good condition. Our cold ice water spilled on me, and Mema had broken her small fingernail. Mema was lying with her head on my lap sound asleep and did not see anything until we got out of the car. Being blessed as we were, the truck in front of us witnessed the accident and told me that he thought I had it under control at one time until one of the trailer outriggers caught the pavement. This trucker was a friend of ours from Berlin, Georgia, Mr. Ronald Roberts, who had married Jackie Liles. We contacted Tom's mother, and she came and took the girls to her home while Tom and I stayed to take care of all the paperwork and dispose of all our stuff. After all was taken care of, Tom and I hitchhiked to his home where the girls had rested and were in much better condition. Mema had contacted her parents, and they had sent us fifty dollars so we could ride the bus for the remainder of the trip. Mema and I finally arrived home, and everyone was so glad to see us and all in one piece. The Lord had truly blessed us on our trip. We spent a few days resting and visiting our relatives and catching up on all the latest gossip. After a few days at home, I had to plan my return trip to Miramar and chose to ride the bus. It was a long and uneventful trip back to the base by myself, but I made it okay.

It was not long before we were deployed to Alaska for the second time, and we did not do anything different the second time that we did the first time. We had all our routine maintenance, pleasure time, and climbing "the old woman," which was a mountain near the base. I climbed the mountain with no problem and had an enjoyable day away from my work. Coming down was more difficult than going up because you could lose your balance and fall a long distance; however, it was fun and just something else to do other than working.

On this deployment, I was selected to be part of the aircrew as a second mechanic. I flew in the tail of the aircraft as an observer who watched the engines in operation. On one of these flights we were just tooling along, taking our pictures as we were supposed to do, when suddenly our pilot received a radio message. The message told us to turn around 180 degrees and fly until further notice. We were unaware that we were flying over Russian territory. This could have been a lot worse due to the time it was and the relationship we had with Russia. I always enjoyed flying as it was so peaceful up twenty-thousand feet in the air just cruising along. It was on this deployment that I received a telegram on August 29, 1954, advising me that I was the proud father of a ten-pound-and-six-ounce baby boy, Larry Leon Eldridge. I had to buy and pass out cigars as it was the custom to do at that time. I was so proud that everyone was okay and all were healthy. At this time there were no abundance of telephones up there or at least that I had access to. The announcement was in our monthly detachment newspaper, and it made me real proud of what Mema had done for us. She had a rough time during her pregnancy, but all was better after the birth of Larry. We can thank the Lord for His blessings and help in taking care of us during the rough times.

Before leaving Alaska, I had applied for leave so I could go home and bring Mema and Larry back with me. I finally decided to hitchhike home instead of riding the bus. I had enough money to ride a bus but thought I could save the money for later. You see, I was tight with a dollar back in my younger years also. To be safe, I put all my money in my shoe except a few dollars and began hitchhiking to Georgia. One of my sailor friends heard about me going to Georgia; and he offered me a ride to Dallas, Texas. This was about halfway home, and it was a blessing within itself. I did not walk hardly any on the way home as I caught rides for long distances throughout the trip. One ride in particular stands out in my mind. I was standing on the roadside in Gettysburg, Mississippi, when a young black man drove by and then stopped. He backed up to me and asked if I wanted to ride with him. I stated that I would, and he just smiled and told me to get in. He pulled into a gas station and filled with gas and checked all fluid levels. He asked me if I could drive, and I told him that I could; then I got in and drove while he slept. He had not slept since he left San Diego, California, about sixteen hours; and that was a long way. I drove for several hours until he awoke and started talking to me. We had a good trip, and he even went out of his way to take me closer to my destination, which was a great gesture on his part as he was heading to South Carolina. Back in the 1950s, there was still a lot of discrimination in the Navy and the rest of the country against blacks and other minorities. I did not agree with the position the superiors took but had to live with it. This young black man was extremely good to me as were my Black shipmates in my squadron. He told me that his family did not like for him to have his picture made with his white shipmates. He told me that his girlfriend once cut a photo in half when she saw a white guy in it. Discrimination was so obvious in those days and even up into the midsixties.

He let me out in Colquitt, Georgia, and it was not long before I caught a ride to Moultrie. I cannot remember how I got to Mema's house, but I did go there as fast as I could to see her and Larry. Larry was such a beautiful and chunky baby. Mema was so proud of him and just beamed when I saw him for the first time; Larry was already six weeks old. We were both so proud of him and thankful that Mema did well after his birth. She had some problems, but she was a great mother and took them all in stride. We had a great reunion with one another, and our vacation was over too soon. We purchased us another car, a 1953 Ford Tudor Sedan, to replace the one I wrecked. I had it checked out and serviced to make the trip to Miramar. Everyone hated to see us go and take our infant baby on such a long trip. Grandmother Matt Norman was the most vocal one and was beside herself about the trip. We packed all our goods in the back seat and trunk and then made a bed for Larry in the back seat. He was very comfortable most of the time, and Mema tended to him as I drove. We had a good trip and made it out there without any problems, thank the Lord.

When we arrived back at the base, we applied for housing on the base and moved in shortly thereafter. We lived in a Quonset hut apartment, which had two bedrooms. It was a small place, but it was adequate for us; and Mema kept it spotless all the time as if it was our 2619 Foxwood Road South home. We purchased us a new TV, a dining-room set, and some other stuff to make it more of a home atmosphere. I applied for the B (night) shift so I could search for a part-time job to help us on our bills and give us a little more to spend on ourselves. It was very tight living for us, but we seemed to be happy just being with each other and our son. We had an envelope for each one of our accounts (car payment, rent, utilities, gas, and groceries); and we could not rob from one or the other as we would be short on one of our bills. We would go to the commissary and purchase our staple groceries and purchase our meats and perishable items at a local market or the base service station.

I soon got a part-time job with Sears in San Diego as a stocking assistant in the catalog department. Shortly afterward, I was transferred to the automotive department as the assistant manager. I enjoyed this job and worked with them until two weeks after I was discharged. We had to move off the base and did not want to stay in San Diego, so we took off for home in early October of 1955. This part-time job allowed us to spend more money on ourselves and not be in such a tight monetary situation, and it also gave us a little extra money to spend on the way home from California.

Our first stop was Uncle Gene and Aunt Mary's home in Boise, Idaho, where he was stationed at March Air Force Base. We stayed there a few days and enjoyed our visit with them, and they surely enjoyed having Larry around, who was a little over a year old at the time. In fact, having Larry around them ignited a desire for them to start their own family, and they did a few months later with the arrival of Dana in August of 1956. We left them in Boise and trucked our way on over to Blytheville, Arkansas, to visit an old Navy buddy of mine. We arrived there only to find that he had gone back to California. We stayed around with his family for a while and then headed on over to Memphis, Tennessee, where another Navy buddy lived. This is the family that I stayed with on the weekends while stationed in Millington. They were very glad to see us, and we stayed there a couple of days. They were proud of our little family. We sent them cards for a few years and then just slacked off. I stayed in contact with their son for a long time. He was stationed with me in Jacksonville, Florida. Mema, Aunt Lynn, and I had dinner with him and his wife, Ann, while Lynn was stationed in Millington. We left Memphis and headed on to Moultrie where all our family was patiently waiting on us to bring Larry and, of course, Virginia home. I tried to get employment in the Moultrie area but to no avail. I went to Marietta, Georgia, where I was hired as a mechanic at Lockheed Aircraft. It was a good job, and we stayed there for ten months. I was also in the Naval reserves there and worked as a plane captain on an R4-D8. I enjoyed flying and went many places with my commanding officer and crew. We had a two-week cruise in Bermuda, which was a lot of fun. After working in this job through the very cold winter and for a length of ten months, I learned of a job opening at Moody Air Force Base in Valdosta, Georgia. I traveled to Valdosta and applied for the job as soon as I could because it was a better place to work and much closer home. I was hired immediately and immediately gave Lockheed a two-week notice. Mema and I sold our home in Smyrna, Georgia, and we rented a small house in Moultrie, Georgia.

I remained in the Naval Reserves in Chamblee, Georgia, and drove from Moultrie to Chamblee for my weekend drills so I could maintain my longevity for retirement. Since it was such a long way to drive to my Naval reserve training in Chamblee, Georgia, in June of 1956, I joined the Air Force Reserves, which met in Moultrie. I was given a promotion the staff sergeant, which was a big deal for me. At least I could keep my longevity going until I could find another Navy activity nearby.

While assigned to this Air Force unit, I was privileged to perform active duty at Charleston AF Base in Charleston, South Carolina; Maxwell AF Base at Montgomery, Alabama; Dobbins AF Base in Atlanta, Georgia; and Moody AF Base in Valdosta, Georgia. After working at Moody for four years and six months, I was hired at the O&R Department in Jacksonville, Florida, on the Naval Air Station as a jet engine mechanic. I soon found an Air Force reserve unit and started attending on a monthly basis. It was not long before I made master sergeant (E7) in a recovery unit at Fernandina Beach, Florida. It got to be such a hassle to get back and forth that I joined the Naval reserves again and was inducted as a chief petty officer (E7). Soon after indoctrination, I joined a flight crew and started flying as a crew member in an old patrol plane, the SP-2E. My station in this aircraft was in the nose. I had the best view of all and could see for many miles as we flew patrols hunting for submarines in the Atlantic Ocean. I operated an electronic device that could detect submarines underwater, and when I would see any indications of activity, I would call out "Mad man" in the microphone over our aircraft intercom. This would alert the navigator to mark our position in the ocean and determine if it was an enemy submarine or a friendly submarine. The Navy sent me to a special electronic school in Willow Grove, Pennsylvania, to increase my proficiency in the operation of this special device.

I wanted a more challenging position in the flight crew, so I applied for the position of flight engineer and was awarded this position. I trained for the position of flight engineer and soon qualified in this position. My responsibility in this position was to monitor all the engine instruments on the flight panel and notify the pilot and copilot of any irregularities in readings. I had to learn all the systems in the aircraft and their functions as well. The instrument panel had many lights, and the good light was green; however, when the red light came on there was trouble in the appropriate system. This would enable me to determine if all systems were operating properly at any given moment. Malfunctions could cause very bad damage to the aircraft and possible failure if not detected in time. From time to time, the pilot would allow me to lower or raise the landing wheels. I was also responsible for assuring that the aircraft had the correct amount of fuel, oil, and alcohol for our mission. During flight, I would maintain records of fuel consumption to assure that all operations were going as planned. We were deployed to Guantanamo Bay, Cuba (Gitmo), on a couple of tours and to Roosevelt Roads in Puerto Rico on a tour. We flew in and out of all the islands in the Caribbean Islands during our deployment.

I did rest and relaxation (R & R) in Saint Thomas and Montego Bay, Jamaica. On my last tour as a flight engineer, we were on our way back from Guantanamo Bay, Cuba, when we had indications that we were losing an engine due to metal contamination problems. We landed at Fort Lauderdale, Florida, to evaluate our problem. I checked the engine over, drained some oil in the problem area, switched electrical wires on two magnetic plugs, and ran the engine on a penalty run. Everything checked out okay, so we proceeded on to Jacksonville Naval Air Station where we were stationed. When we were in the landing pattern, I notified the pilot that our engine was going out, and he shut it off and feathered the propeller so we could land in balance. We landed without incident, and the engine crew had to change our engine due to a large amount of metal contamination. I flew in this position until I was promoted to warrant officer on December 15, 1968. Subsequent to my promotion, I was assigned to a squadron as a maintenance officer, which I held for several years. I was deployed to Rota, Spain, on a couple of tours and enjoyed the area very much. This friend of mine stationed over there took me out to the good eateries for some special local cuisine. It was all very delicious even though I did not know what I was eating.

Due to rotation duty, I was assigned to the Naval Reserve Center as a recruiting officer and stayed there until 1971 where I had received several awards for our "outstanding" recruiting efforts. During this time, I recruited Larry into the Naval reserves, Aunt Lynn into the Naval reserves, and our neighbor Mr. Jim Davis into the Naval reserves. In 1971 I found a home in a unit at Wing-11 and stayed there until I retired in October 6, 1991. It was a mandatory retirement as I did not want to retire from a job I loved so much.

I drilled in the capacity of maintenance officer for twenty years and loved every bit of it. I was deployed to many places and accompanied the Wing-11 commodore on several occasions to Bermuda, Iceland, and Sicily. I enjoyed my tour with the Wing-11 staff, and they were very gracious to me and allowed me to act upon my own free will in making decisions about supply, logistics, and maintenance problems. On many occasions I would sit in for the maintenance officer while he was absent for one reason or another. Active duty personnel do not normally attend retirement ceremonies for reservists; however, I had several high-ranking officers attend mine and wish me "God's speed and good luck." My commanding officer made a statement just prior to piping Mema and me over the side (this was when you walk down between two rows of your shipmates that are honoring you and your spouse): "I have retired many military personnel with twenty years of service. However, never one with forty years of service." I miss my Navy friends very much and hear from some of them from time to time, and they always appear glad to hear from me.

The following is a copy of the letter of appreciation I received from the commodore of my active-duty command upon my retirement from the Naval reserves. It was only by the grace of God that I was able to achieve the things that I did. Without His help, I could have done nothing.

One of the most humbling experiences that I have ever had was in a Walmart in Fleming Island, Florida. I was walking in the store with my retired Navy cap on when two small children, ages five and seven, came up to me with extended hands and wanted to thank me for my service in the military. Then their three-year-old sibling and their mother did the same. I almost lost it right there as my emotions were at their highest level ever in a situation such as this. I talked with them for a short while and assured them that it was all my pleasure for serving my country.

I will list my duty stations so you will understand that Papa did travel in a lot of foreign countries. I did not stay in some of them very long but enjoyed representing my country the best I could. These are not listed in sequence but randomly.

Guantanamo Bay Naval Station, Cuba (several times)
Roosevelt Roads Naval Station, Puerto Rico
Bermuda Naval Station (several times)
Lodges Naval Station; Azores, Greece (several times)
Keflavik Naval Station; Keflavik, Iceland
Upper Harford Station in England near London
Kodiak and Fairbanks Alaska (before it was a state)
Rota Naval Station; Rota, Spain (several times)
Naval Station in Sigonella, Sicily

Copenhagen, Denmark
Naples, Italy
Canal Zone, South America
Montego Bay, Jamaica

MY FAMILY MILITARY SERVICE

BY HOMER J. ELDRIDGE

I have researched as thoroughly as I could, and I have found no evidence that any of my relatives served in the Civil War. I am still researching the issue and, hopefully, will come to an opinion soon. I have no record of my great-grandfather, Reacie Layton John Thomas Eldridge; my grandfathers, Homer Jackson Eldridge or Augustus Hodge; or my father, Everett Preston Eldridge, having served in any military branch at all. From that era until today, we have had many relatives serve and die in national conflicts. Several of our relatives served and died in Europe during World War II, the Korean War, the Vietnam Conflict, the Iraq Invasion of 1992, and the Iraq and Afghanistan Conflict of 2002 to 2011.

After her divorce from our father, our mother met and married a chief in the Navy named Harold Ormston, a prince of a gentleman. He saw plenty of action during World War II but was not one to talk much about it to the family. He retired in 1953 after serving thirty-three years in the Navy. He and Mother lived together until she died on September 3, 1986. After he became ill, he moved to Orange Park, Florida, and lived with us until he was checked into an assisted-living home where he died on October 15, 1992.

After graduation Betty left home in December 1949 and went to Key West, Florida, to live with our mother who had married a chief in the Navy. After being in Key West for a while, Betty married a sailor named Jabe Sherertz in 1951. He served in the Navy for many years aboard ship and as an instructor in the Naval Sonar School in

Key West, Florida, where he retired in 1966. After retirement, Jabe became a dock master at Key West Yacht Club. Betty and Jabe lived together for many years and had three children. They divorced in 1979. She married again on February 14, 1981, to Jack Burke. Jack was good to Betty, and they lived together until his death on July 28, 2007. Jack served in World War II in the Army Air Corps as a gunner in a patrol bomber. On one of his missions, he and his pilot were the only survivors to return to their base. After the war, he switched over to the Navy and served with them until he retired in 1959 after twenty years of combined service. He was a very patriotic man and loved his country by serving in some special veteran organizations up until a few months prior to his death.

I left home and joined the Navy on October 4, 1951, and was shipped off to San Diego, California, in a short time. I guess Daddy missed me since I was his eldest son and he had trained me to do more farming chores than the others. The next year Daddy purchased a tractor to replace me and the mules, Frank and Lady. I remained in the regular Navy and Naval reserves until October 6, 1991, a total of forty years and two days. I served four years in the regular Navy. While there, I served three tours overseas: two in Kodiak, Alaska, and one in Panama Canal Zone. During this time, I flew in an SNJ twin-engine aircraft and a PB4Y/2P (a World War II patrol bomber). The Air Force called this aircraft a B24 Bomber, which was utilized extensively in bombing the Germans and Japanese from high altitudes. Upon being released from active duty in September 1955, I joined the Naval Air reserves and served in Atlanta, Georgia, until July 1957. At which time I joined the Air Force reserves to be near home for my reserve duty. During this time, I attained the rank of master sergeant. After moving to Jacksonville, Florida, in 1960 to a new job at the Naval Air station, I switched back over to the Naval Air reserves in 1963 as a chief petty officer. I flew as a flight engineer in a P2V-2 Neptune aircraft until being commissioned a warrant officer on December 15, 1968. I remained as a warrant officer until I retired as a CWO-4 on October 6, 1991. As a reservist maintenance officer working for the commodore of ComPatWing-11 Jacksonville, I flew to many foreign places such as Naval Station Guantanamo, Cuba;

Naval Station Roosevelt Roads, Puerto Rico; Naval Station Lagos, Portugal; Naval Station Rota, Spain; Naval Station Bermuda Island; Naval Station Sigonella, Sicily; Naval Station Keflavik, Iceland; and Naval Station Bermuda. I also flew to many places within the United States while a flight engineer in the P2V-2P on training missions. When I retired, my commanding officer told the audience that he had retired many sailors with twenty years of service but never one with over forty years of service. It was a great honor for me to have done so well, and I thanked the Lord for this feat and not anything I had done. He had blessed me to fly many missions of service over land and over the seas and brought me safely back home each time. I am not saying that we never had any problems; however, our training and ability to rectify the problems brought us home safe. We had lost engines on occasions but were blessed to fly home to complete our mission and file the reports. In November of 1970 we established a new squadron of P-3 patrol aircraft in what is now VP-62. I was later transferred from this squadron due to the lack of a billet job position to another active reserve squadron of which I was a recruiting officer for several years.

Gene was the next to leave home for one reason or another. He joined the Air Force on June 1954 and served all over the world for twenty-six years. He attained the rank of captain and retired in 1982. Gene went to basic training at Lowery Air Force Base in Denver, Colorado. He met and married Mary Hassig, and they had three children. Gene went to electronic school and learned all about stray ohms and aircraft electronics. He performed maintenance on many of the Air Force aircraft during his enlisted tenure and traveled all over the world doing so. He attended college, earned an engineering degree, and was commissioned as a first lieutenant in the Air Force. After retirement, he worked for Lockheed Missile Division in Colorado as an engineer.

James L. Hart Jr., our stepbrother, joined the Navy on September 28, 1955, and was stationed in San Diego, California, at the same time I was there and was discharged there on September 25, 1959. JL worked on aircraft engines in the Navy and was very good at his job. JL was very quick to learn whatever he wanted to learn and was highly proficient at performing his task. He met and married Lola Hattie Kite in San Diego. They eventually had four children and were divorced in 1968. He was married a couple of other times and had children by one of them. Subsequent to his discharge, JL worked as an automobile mechanic for many years. He was one of the best ones I ever saw. JL died on December 27, 2004, and had no spouse or children with him at that time.

Pat joined the Air Force in June 1956 and served all over the world for twenty-two years. This included two tours in Vietnam at Da Nang. He attained the rank of senior master sergeant at which he retired in 1972. While he was stationed at Kessler Air Force Base, he married Clarice May, a student nurse, from Berlin. After their marriage, Clarice finished nursing school, and then they went through the ceremony again as she was not supposed to marry while a student. While stationed in Germany in 1974, he and Clarice collected many artifacts from there, and they still have most of them. During this time Mema, Aunt Betty, Aunt Lynn, and I visited them and had a great two weeks in the surrounding countries as well as visiting the castles in the local area.

Kenneth joined the Army in 1964 and served eighteen months with most of that in Korea. He was discharged in May 1966 and returned home. Betty's son-in-law, Bobby Doyle, served in the Navy. He was married to Aunt Betty's daughter, Patti. I enlisted my daughter, Aunt Lynn, into the Naval reserves in 1983, and she served for several years; part of that was overseas in Spain. Her commitment to other things caused her to leave the reserves in 1985. I also enlisted my son, Larry (Gramps), into the Navy in 1981; and he served in the Seabees for four years until and injury disqualified him for service. He was discharged in 1986. Pat's son, David, enlisted in the Army reserves. He obtained his master's degree in history and was commissioned as a first lieutenant. He has traveled to many parts of the world in his field of expertise. At the time of this writing, he remains in the active Army reserves and currently holds the rank of lieutenant colonel. He served in Iraq and/or Afghanistan. Pat's youngest son, Scott, served in the Army in the 101st Airborne Division. He also served in the first Iraq invasion in 1992. Pat's grandson, Donnie Eldridge, joined the Air Force in 2005 and is still serving as of today. He is an aircraft engine mechanic for the F-15 fighter jets. He has served in Afghanistan and other foreign countries as well. As one can see, our family has served the military very well and can be pleased that we have done our part of protecting our country in one way or another no matter what our job was. None of the ones mentioned above has ever had any disciplinary problems and served their country in a very patriotic manner.

Note: It is very difficult for many young people to understand that success did not come overnight or in thirty minutes as shown on TV. Most successful people started out with very little or nothing at all, as Mema and I did. One has to work for the good things in life and must realize that everything was not handed down on a platter, so to speak. Hopefully, there is a story in this writing and it may inspire someone to understand that it takes patience, love, hard work, understanding, trust in one another, and a blessing from God to achieve anything significant in life. As the old saying goes, "There are no free lunches." Someone has to pay—maybe not the recipient but someone else.

OUR HUMBLE BEGINNING

After our short honeymoon was over, Mema and I went back to her home to stay for the remainder of my leave. Since I was going back overseas, Mema stayed home with her parents to finish high school and graduate with her classmates.

Mema and I were married on April 25, 1953, in her home with many friends and relatives present. As usual, after a wedding, a couple normally takes a honeymoon of some sort. Mema and took a short one in an apartment borrowed from my Aunt Pansy Meadows, my dad's sister who lived in Moultrie. Her husband was overseas, so she volunteered this apartment. It was a nice gesture, and we did appreciate it very much as we did not have enough money for a motel or any other long period of time.

After I finished my tour in Alaska, Mema came to California by train to reunite with me. I and my friends, Jim and Earlene Swanson, had already found us an apartment. It was a small upstairs apartment in Escondido near our friend's home. Mema was not exactly pleased that she did not help select our home. We stayed there a short time, and Mema chose to move downstairs to another apartment. We lived in this downstairs apartment for a short time and then moved over to another single apartment in the same compound; however, it was an independent apartment, and we were all by ourselves in the corner of the lot. It was in this apartment that Mema became pregnant with Larry, and we were very happy. This apartment was furnished with a gas stove, and the smell made Mema very sick. At this time, we chose to move closer to the base where I was stationed, and our trailer was on the base where I had been in boot camp training a few months ago. This trailer was not as nice as our apartment, but we were happy to be alone with each other. It was just across from my work area, and it did not take me very long to get home to my newly pregnant wife. Our trailer was a small pull-behind vehicle that measured eight feet wide by twenty-seven feet long. It was a very small and crowded place with no room for us to pass each other in the hall. Mema was sick at times; and when I heard her yelp, I knew to get out of her way because she was on her way to the bathroom to throw up. This was just a ritual for us, and I always felt so bad for her; however, she never complained about the inconvenience.

It was time for me to go back overseas, so I had to get Mema back home so she could be with her parents when Larry was born. We did not want her to be alone in California when she gave birth to Larry. We packed everything we had in a trailer and in the trunk of our 1950 Ford and started home along with our friends Tommy and Rosie. Rosie was about two more weeks pregnant than Mema, and she was also going home to give birth to her baby as well.

Everything was going well until we came upon some construction between Midland and Odessa, Texas. There were no warnings or markings on the construction site, and we had the misfortune of hitting some of it and wrecking our car. Our car rolled over at least once and was facing in the opposite direction from whence we came. The Lord blessed all of us as none of us were hurt and both women were in good condition despite our accident. Tommy called his mother who lived about two hours away, and she came to get the girls. Tommy and I stayed and took care of all paperwork, and then we went to his mother's as well. Virginia's parents, Ola and Wheeler Norman, sent us enough money to ride a bus home from Texas. We arrived home okay and had a great visit before I had to catch the bus back to Miramar Naval Air Station for shipment overseas to Alaska for the second time.

Larry was born on August 28, 1954, and I received a telegram advising me that all were doing just fine along with all the stats about the birth. (Remember, we did not have access to telephones at that time, so telegrams were the in thing.) After my deployment was over in September, I went on leave and hitchhiked home. I hitchhiked

2,600 miles to get to my Mema and my small baby boy, Larry. While home we had to purchase a car since we wrecked our other one on the way home. We drove back to Miramar, and we rented a small apartment in La Jolla, California, until we could rent one on the base. Our new home on base was a half-round Quonset hut. It was a two-bedroom apartment and was not a very large place at all. It was our home, and we enjoyed it very much. This is the place where we bought our first television and first furniture. I started working part-time for Sears in San Diego shortly after returning back to our base and worked there until two weeks after I was discharged in September 30, 1955.

After discharge, we headed back to Georgia. Our first stop was in Boise, Idaho, where Gene and Mary were stationed. We visited them for several days and had a wonderful time as always. They enjoyed playing with Larry and decided that they wanted a child of their own to play with. That was October of 1955, and Dana was born in August of 1956. Our next stop was in Blytheville, Arkansas, to visit one of my old shipmates. He had gone back to California, so we did not tarry there very long and headed to Memphis, Tennessee, to visit Mom and Dad Compagna. These folks took me in while I was stationed at Millington and treated as one of their own. I was good buddies with their son while stationed at Jacksonville, Florida Naval Air Station at AN (P) School in 1952. We stayed a couple of days and enjoyed our visit very much, and they enjoyed Larry as well. We left there and came to Moultrie to start our hunt for a job.

We could not find a job in Moultrie, so we went to Atlanta to apply. I was hired by Lockheed Aircraft Company on my first day in Atlanta as an aircraft engine mechanic. Mema and I rented a small upstairs apartment near the base until we could find a home to purchase. We rented for one month, and then we purchased a new home on Old Concord Road South in Smyrna, Georgia. This was a small three-bedroom home but was very comfortable for us. We must have been complacent and comfortable in that environment because Lynn was conceived there within a month or so, which made us very happy. We enjoyed our home for a while, but we wanted to move near Moultrie. I applied for a job at Moody AFB and was hired immediately. We sold our home in Smyrna and moved in with Mom and Dad Norman. Then we rented a small home in Moultrie; however, it was over fifty miles to work each way, and this was expensive for us. We remodeled one of Dad Norman's farmhouses and moved into it, and this put me fifteen miles nearer to my job at Moody. During the remodeling, we put a bathroom in this home as it only had an outhouse prior to that. Larry and Lynn had their own room; but we had no air-conditioning, and the only heat was an open wood-burning fireplace. We would make sure that Larry and Lynn were very well covered up in the winter, and Mema would get up during the night to check on them being covered up and comfortable. All in all, we were happy living in this little home, and Larry loved it because he loved being near his grandparents and they loved doing things for him. After a couple of years in the farmhouse, we purchased a small home in Valdosta on Jane Street and enjoyed it for a while. We were neighbors to John and Nina Butts, whom we still stay in contact with from time to time. Larry and Lynn had the measles while living here. In a couple of years, we wanted a larger home; so we purchased a home on Lausanne Street, which was only a couple of streets over from Jane Street. While living in Valdosta, I worked at a Gulf service station part-time in the afternoons to boost our income. It seems that I always had a second job to help boost our income.

I received word from the employment office at Moody that many civilians were being released due to the change in our mission, so we had to sell our sweet little home. It did not take us long to sell it because we had taken good care of this home that was painted yellow and trimmed with brown paint. It looked like a gingerbread house. Once we sold the home, we rented a home from Mr. Nichols that was in front of the old air base, Spence Field. We lived in this house for six months to complete our employment at Moody on November 16, 1960. After being notified that I would be terminated on November 16, 1960, I applied for and was hired at the overhaul facility on Jacksonville Naval Station. I was to begin my employment on Monday after being terminated on Friday. The Lord blessed our family very much as this was the best move I had ever made in my employment career.

I began working in the jet engine repair shop. I was shortly transferred to the engine test division where I tested the newly over-hauled reciprocating and jet engines to make sure they would with-stand full operation in the fleet. I performed this duty for about three years, and then I was transferred to the engine component overhaul section. These components were used on many engines and aircraft for the Navy and Air Force. I was soon transferred to the bearing section where I worked for about six months before being promoted to the material office as an assistant planner and estimator in support of the Navy and the Air Force. During this time, I was attending Saint Johns River Junior College in Palatka, Florida, toward a degree in business.

As a side note to this epistle, after moving to Jacksonville, I worked part-time at three different shipping companies. I started off at Sea Land Trucking. In about six months, I moved to Alderman's Transport Company where I worked for about a year or so. At this company I worked from forty to sixty hours per week and worked at least forty hours at the Naval Air Station. The company was very good to me and shifted my work hours to accommodate my hours at the Naval Air Station Jacksonville. I was promoted to night manager where I loaded and unloaded trucks traveling through our terminal to other destinations. During this time, I was also performing my duty in the Air Force and Naval Air reserves on certain weekends and active duty tours around the world. This statement is provided to make the reader aware of how much Mema and I worked and sacri-ficed to provide for our family and give them many things that they wanted and not only the things we could afford at that time. It is not easy to work the long hours that we did, and we knew that our suc-cess would not always be the easiest road to travel. I would work at NAS until 11:00 PM and check-in at Alderman's around 11:20 PM to commence my work there. I would leave there and come home to Mema's breakfast, which would be ready for me. I would eat, shower, and sleep until around 2:30 PM then get ready for my job at NAS. It was all to do again the next day, and this continued for over a year.

Mema was concerned that I was working all the time, so she suggested that she get a job and I start college as soon as Lynn started to school, In December of 1962, Mema was hired at Montgomery Ward in the layaway department and worked there until January 1964. In January of 1964, Mema applied for and was hired as a bookkeeper at Dixie Egg on Edgewood Court. In May of 1964, she was hired at Winn-Dixie, also as a bookkeeper, and worked there until October of 1987. Also during this time, I went to school and obtained my Florida contractor's license and, later, my Florida roofing contractor's license. I built custom homes during the evenings and weekends. I exerted my efforts to building homes at an affordable rate. I did this from 1972 until 1997 when we moved from Florida back to Georgia. This was after Mom Norman passed away on January 5, 1997.

In about a year or so, I was promoted to planner and estimator in support of the J52 jet engine. During this position, I traveled to many places in support of this program. After working in this office for about a year or so, I was transferred to the workload division to gain additional experience for future positions in this facility. During most of the last three years, I served as vice president and president of our local P & E association. This organization represented all members of the planners and estimators and progress men. I traveled to Washington, DC, and other places to perform business for these employees. Fortunately, I did well in all positions assigned and was soon promoted to the high position of supervisory planner and estimator where I served for about six years moonlighting the performance of many employees supporting the Navy and the Air Force. Subsequent to my tenure in this position, I was transferred to the position of supervisory aircraft examiner where I became the highest blue-collar employee on the Naval Air Station.

From this position, I was promoted in 1982 to the position of the Fleet Readiness Action Group (FRAG) director, GS-12. I supervised many employees, both civilian and military, in the support of our Naval fleet and the Air Force. I retired from this position in May 1, 1987.

I remained in the Naval Air reserves all this time; and on December 15, 1968, I was promoted to chief warrant officer 4. I filled the position of aircraft maintenance officer in my reserve squadron and at the Wing-11 logistic division. This position supported all the P-3 aircraft, which is a sophisticated patrol aircraft, the community, and the P-3 training squadron. I remained in this position until October 6, 1991, at which time I retired from the Navy with forty years and two months and a few days of active duty and reserve service, of which I am very grateful.

After retirement from civil service, I continued to build and reroof homes in Duval, Clay, and Baker Counties until September 1992. Hurricane Andrew devastated the Miami, Florida, area so I went there to work for a large construction company out of Jasper, Florida. I worked in that area until September of 1993 and then returned to Orange Park, Florida, to continue my construction trades in the local area. I worked there until Grandma Norman passed away on January 5, 1997. Mema inherited the old home place, so we sold our home in Foxwood and moved to Georgia for, hopefully, our final move.

Since our return to the farm, Mema and I have reestablished our roots in the neighborhood and Colquitt County and have hopefully made a difference in the county and our community. We are known very well in the surrounding counties and among our Primitive Baptist churches and all their members.

I have continued my construction company in Georgia and have accomplished the rework of homes in several counties surrounding Moultrie. We also continue to upgrade our old home place by remodeling and adding on to the original house built by Grandpa Norman in 1942. We have also upgraded our farm by reconstructing the ponds and by clearing out much of the old trees and shrubbery around its perimeter. In 2008 we built a two-bedroom cottage near our home for our boys to stay in while they visited us from time to time. We always enjoy our boys when they come to visit, and they all appear to have a great time in Georgia and especially on the farm. All of them love to fish and hunt the game that is found on our farm. It is a great place for them to release their anxieties and learn to drive various vehicles without the threat of endangering too many people. During all this time, Mema and I had worked very hard to provide our family with faith, love, and stability. We always attended and supported our church and visited other churches as well. We wanted to be a good solid family and a good neighbor to all that needed us.

Note: I would be remiss if I did not include this article in my book to my boys to let them be aware of where I received my desire and determination of my work ethics. As you will see, my dad was a special person because he instilled in each of his children to work hard for the things they desired or dreamed about. He did not believe that the government owed us a living, and none of were ever on welfare or any government subsidies.

MY DAD, A
HARDWORKING MAN

My dad, Everett Preston Eldridge, was born on July 6, 1915, in Worth County, Georgia, and died on August 13, 2000, at his home near Berlin, Georgia.

There are many sides to every person, and they are seen differently by everyone they come in contact with, especially their family. Dad was born in a poor family, and he was the first child of Homer Jackson Eldridge and Leila (Eldridge) Eldridge. His mother died of pneumonia when he was about two years old; she had been looking for him outside when it was raining and caught cold. And consequently, it turned into pneumonia. Many times, my father blamed himself for her death.

He was taught to work hard at an early age and continued to do so throughout his entire life almost up until his death. His last job was with the Southwest Georgia Community Council at which he worked until they finally made him stop coming to the office.

Early in life, when he was about eleven years old, his dad was injured by a log and was unable to work for a long time. Dad had to quit school to help tend the farm that his dad was a sharecropper on. He never returned to school to finish so he ended up with a fourth-grade education. He continued to work on the farm, and after several years. he met and married (on January 31, 1931) Anna Malinda Hodge from Dooley County, Georgia. Shortly after they were married, Daddy and Mother moved to Orlando, Florida, where he worked in the orange groves doing maintenance. Later that year, my sister, Betty, was born on December 11, 1931. Daddy continued to work in the orange groves in Orange County, Florida, until they moved to a better job in Polk County, Florida, doing basically the same type of work. Daddy worked there and carved out a living doing anything possible to make enough money for them to live on.

Daddy found out that Mother was pregnant with me, and he knew he had to get a better job other than orange grove work. Daddy told me, on one of our trips to Mayo Clinic in Jacksonville, Florida, that when he found out that Mother was pregnant with me, he got off his tractor one afternoon and knelt down by his tire and prayed for a better job. He told the Lord that he needed a better job so he could provide for his family. I was born on September 28, 1933, and shortly thereafter, a hurricane came through Polk County and wiped out everything he owned. My mother could tell that I was close to being born, so she sent my father for the doctor. While he was gone, I decided to come into this world without a doctor. My grandfather, Homer Eldridge, being the only other person at home with my mother, assisted my mother with my delivery. Since he did all that for them, they let him name me; and of course, he named me after himself. Three days after I was born, Daddy and Mother moved back to Orange County, Florida, where he had arranged to work for a contractor building houses. This paid much more money than the orange grove maintenance did, and it would help with a wife and two children to take care of now. Daddy worked very hard to learn the carpenter trade and also learn as much as he could so he could advance in the business. Out of the clear blue sky one afternoon, his employer asked him if he wanted a commission on the house they had just sold. Of course Daddy replied to the positive. His employer gave him a hundred-dollar bonus for doing a good job. He said that had never happened to him before.

However, he was much smarter than his fourth-grade education and smarter than many with a high school education as he normally used common sense in most of his decisions. He could figure standing lumber in trees and also calculate the materials required to build buildings, lay out trusses on buildings, lay out steps, and cut finished material as good as the next person and better than most. He had an aptitude for math and used it wisely and efficiently. He was in the construction trade most of his life and assisted in building large buildings as well as homes. One notable large building is the old Coca-Cola plant in Moultrie, Georgia.

My brother, Everett (Gene) was born on June 15, 1936; and on July 26, 1938, my younger brother, Reasie (Pat), was born. Both were born in Orange County, Florida, not far from each other's birthplace since we had moved to a larger home near the Sangsters Lilly Farm subsequent to Gene being born. Dad continued to work in carpentry as well as working in the groves part-time to have additional income.

Daddy was unable to join the Army because of an old injury but was drafted into the corps of engineers for the duration of World War II, which ended in June of 1945.

Daddy would work three jobs to make ends meet and to provide us with the things we needed. He would arise around 3:00 AM each day to deliver the *Orlando Sentinel* newspaper in Orlando, Florida. Then he would go to the Army base and work full-time there building for the Army by blocking and bracing the equipment being shipped overseas and to the other parts of the country. Many times, he would work overtime, and this would cut into his time of rest before his other job maintaining buildings for a Mr. Proctor who had apartments on Lake Sunset near our home in the suburbs of Orlando.

Even though Daddy was working so hard to make our life easier, he had time to do special things for others, especially children. Daddy always made an effort to have us something special for Christmas and wanted other children to have the same. He spent many hours at the Salvation Army Center assuring that other children had toys and candy. He would pass out toys and candy to the ones coming to the joyous occasion and to those that were less fortunate than us. I can remember going to the Salvation Army Hall with Daddy, Betty, Gene, and Pat, who was really an infant at that time.

He built our home in Orlando mostly by himself as he had nobody else to assist him during the hours he needed them. I do remember our mother helping him install the ceiling boards. He would place the large sheets up in position, and Mother would place a "preacher" or a "dead man" in position to hold the material until Daddy could nail it into place. The "dead man" was a long stick with a four-foot piece nailed at one end as to make a cross, which would support the material without much strain on his assistant, who was our mother, Anne.

After Mother and Daddy divorced in September 1940, Daddy was much busier trying to tend to four children and make a living for all of us. My grandfather, Homer, lived with us and assisted Daddy in caring for us as best possible. In fact, Granddaddy was with us more than Daddy because he was working so much. During this time, Daddy would take Betty and me to Georgia for the summer to stay with some of our relatives who had other children for us to work and play with. It was during one of these visits that he went to a local peanut boil at a neighbor's home near Uncle Clarence Mims' and met our future stepmother, Thelma Gertrude (Hart) Hart. It was a whirlwind romance; and not long after they met, they were married on May 30, 1942, in Colquitt County, Georgia. She had a son, James L. Hart Jr., by a previous marriage, which had ended with the death of her first husband. Her and her son moved to Orlando where all the fun began for the stepchildren. This brought a new meaning to Daddy working hard. He worked harder trying to keep the marriage going than anything else. No matter how hard he tried, nothing was going right for her and her son in a home filled with Eldridges and our grandfather, Homer. It was a difficult time for all of us, not knowing her or her son and trying to maintain a balance between doing the correct thing for everyone and working for a living as well. Daddy really had a hard time balancing everything to suit her, JL, and all his children as well. I can look back now and realize how much stress and mental pressure he was under never knowing when Thelma would be there or gone. It had to be a tremendous burden; however, I do not remember him running around in a tizzy. Once World War II was over, the government released Daddy from his contracting job so he could do whatever he wished. First of all, he purchased a new one-ton Chevrolet truck for us to move to Georgia in. We watched him build the large truck body while the frame was resting on four large drums. Of all things for him to do, he bought a farm in Colquitt County, Georgia, near the small town of Berlin. We moved there in December of 1945 with Daddy and me bringing all our animals to the farm during the Christmas holidays. After we unloaded the animals, I stayed with our uncle Artie and aunt Evie Tompkins while Daddy went back to Orlando so he could bring our furniture and the rest of the family to our new home. It was a strange feeling being in this new place where we had never been before without all the things we were accustomed to in Orlando. One has to understand that in December 1945, my sister, Betty, was fourteen years old; I was twelve years old; my brother, Gene, was nine years old; and my baby brother, Pat, was seven years old. Betty and I are the only ones that had stayed in Georgia for any length of time. All of us children were in a foreign land knowing hardly anyone at all.

Daddy began his new career as a farmer, and it was a big change for him and all the rest of the family. It was a drastic change from his former job and much more demanding. Farming required working from daylight until dark and even longer in some cases. Daddy learned his new trade through the school of hard knocks, trial and error, and just plain old persistence. He taught me to do many things as he went along learning himself. He did have several of the older farmers in the neighborhood that would help him when he asked for assistance in a particular job that he wanted to do, namely Uncle Artie Tompkins (on my granddaddy's side), Uncle Bonds Strickland (on my stepmother's side), and Mr. Benton Flowers, just a good neighbor.

Daddy tried many different kinds of crops during the next few years, but tobacco and cotton were our stable crops. Not being a seasoned farmer, Daddy did pretty well the first few years of farming. He worked hard and made sure that I did also. He taught me how to plow the mules and horses as needed. I would turn land with either animal, or he would use the remaining animal or animals. There was a lot of walking as we did not have a tractor to make things easier. We would turn the land about six to eight inches at a round, level it out for planting with a drag harrow, and then we would plant our crops or make land beds to transplant our young plants in.

Daddy would work hard for nine months, and then in the fall and winter, he would go to Columbus, Georgia, to work in construction so he could make money for us to live on the next year without borrowing from the banks. He would work long hours while in Columbus, making all the money he could as he knew it would take it to keep us in food and clothing.

Daddy planted a lot of different crops trying to find one that was a cash crop, but he just never made a big hit on anything but tobacco and sometimes cotton. We did most all the work on the farm, and Daddy would never hire any work done because he had us there to assist him in all the chores. It took all of us to accomplish the tasks as we would work before school and after school to keep up with the duties laid out for us by Daddy. In addition to the other chores assigned to us, Betty and I milked our cows each morning and afternoon; this would supply us with fresh milk for household use. We would eventually make buttermilk and butter from the old milk that we did not drink. Farming was a tough and work-related business during our earlier years.

On October 4, 1951, I joined the Navy and was shipped off in a short time. Daddy really missed me as I was his oldest son and could do much more than any of the others because I had the training. The next year before the farming begun, Daddy purchased a tractor to replace me and the mules. Daddy continued to farm for many more years, and one by one, five of his sons joined the military to make a career of their own.

Soon after all his sons left him alone on the farm, he sold it to one of his stepnephews. He only kept enough land for his home and Ray's home, my half brother. He continued to work for the Southwest Community Council until they would not let him work anymore.

However, this did not stop Daddy from doing the thing he loved most: carpentering. Daddy took on the job of remodeling the Berlin Baptist Church in Berlin, Georgia. He had to work with whatever help he could get from volunteers, and it was a great challenge. They tore down the old sanctuary and cleared the spot so they could rebuild in the same area. He helped clean all the savable lumber and neatly stored it in a suitable place for reuse. He designed the new sanctuary and made a pattern for the new roof trusses. He reused the old lumber first prior to buying any new lumber. This would cut cost dramatically. After much laboring with his "help," he finally had the roof back on. The other work progressed very well, and finally, the church was ready to trim out. I was told that Daddy trimmed the entire interior of the church by himself because he wanted it done right. The interior of that church stands today as a monument of what one person can do with a little determination. When we visit the Berlin Baptist Church from time to time, we have to look around to see the great finishing-trim work of our father; and we are proud of his accomplishments.

Even after his retirement from his scheduled job, he continued to do various carpentry and electrical jobs for friends and neighbors. Daddy used mostly all old-type tools and never converted to many of the more modern and faster tools of the trade. I remember him unfolding and folding his old measuring "folding tape" after each use and sticking it in his apron. He took great pride in all his tools and kept them in top condition for more efficient use. I have seen him sharpen his handsaw and set the teeth many times and remove any rust that may have accumulated on it. His saw would cut smooth and efficient each time he used it. He kept his framing square and T square in top shape by sanding them and putting oil on them to reduce the chance of rust or corrosion. Each tool had a place in his handmade tool box, and nobody took a chance to borrow or misuse his tools. Daddy was very particular about whom he let borrow or use his tools, and that person had darn better respect their use and upkeep. Daddy worked until he was about eighty-two years old and had worked around power tools for many years. He was very careful while handling these tools; and when he retired or quit working, he had all his fingers, which were a testament to his safety awareness of moving blades. He had witnessed many accidents during his working career, and that was not a pleasant sight to witness.

Finally, he was at a time in his life that he just did not want to do anything. His health had deteriorated to the point that he had lots of doctor's appointments and treatments scheduled, and it took up a lot of his time just keeping up with the appointments. Various ones would take him to the appointments as he could not drive as he once did. I took him to Thomasville Cancer Center several times as well as to the Mayo Clinic in Jacksonville, Florida. I would also take him to the Pain Management Centers in Jacksonville when he had an infected place on one of his ankles that would not heal. It was during one of these visits that I almost coldcocked a doctor for mashing his ankle too hard. Dad could withstand a lot of pain, and all he would do was grimace with pain and look dreadful at the time.

It was during these trips that he told me many things that we had never discussed before, lots of stories of all the children and his family. I believe he knew that he was nearing the end of his life on earth, but he never fretted about it to me. In fact, he told me on several occasions that he did not fear death at all. The doctors told us that Daddy did not have long to live and that we should call all the family and tell them so. He was nonresponsive for several days, and all his children were present except Gene who lived in Colorado and was on his way home. Although Daddy would not respond to anything we said, we would lean over and assure him that Gene was on his way to see him; and we also told him that we loved him and wanted him to hang in there for a while. He would not have a serious reaction, but we almost knew he understood the things that we were telling him.

Gene and his wife, Mary, finally arrived prior to Daddy passing, and we think it was a blessing for all of us. At that time, we gave Gene and Mary private time to talk with Daddy and to say what they wanted to say or to tell him, and hopefully, he would understand. We told him that all his family was present and that it would be okay to let go. It is amazing how Daddy held on to life in his normal determined way until all his family was present. Not long after their visit with him, he sighed a breath of relief and went to be with the Lord just that quick.

I can honestly say that I have known very few men in my life that worked as hard as my daddy did, and nobody had a bigger determination to perform their job any better than he did. He was truly one of the last of his era. With no known military veterans in our prior three generations, Daddy's family did okay for themselves and made a major contribution to our country. Four of my five brothers and I served in a military capacity in one way or another. Both of my brothers-in-law were retired Navy. My stepdad, three of my nephews, my son, and my daughter also served in the military. All of this is noted below.

After graduating from high school, Betty left home in December 1949 and went to Key West, Florida, to live with our mother who had married a chief in the Navy. After being in Key West for a while, Betty married a sailor named Jabe Sherertz. I left home and joined the Navy on October 4, 1951, where I remained in the regular Navy and Naval reserves until October 6, 1991—a total of forty years and two days. I went from a seaman recruit at recruiting time to CWO-4 at retirement.

Gene was the next one to leave home for one reason or another. He joined the Air Force in June 1954 and served all over the world for twenty-six years. He attained the rank of captain at which he retired in 1972. James L. Hart Jr., our stepbrother, joined the Navy on September 28, 1955, and was stationed in San Diego, California, at the same time I was and was discharged there on September 25, 1959. Pat joined the Air Force in January 4, 1957, and served all over the world for twenty years. This included a tour in Vietnam at Phan Rang AB; in 1967, he was stationed in Germany where he served in accounting and as the isolated unit recreation officer in Germany and England. His last assignment was at Charleston AFB where he was the deputy finance officer. He attained the rank of senior master sergeant at which he retired on May 31, 1980.

Kenneth joined the Army in 1964 and served eighteen months, with most of that was in Korea. He was discharged in May 1966 and returned home.

After her divorce from Jabe Sherertz, Betty married another retired Navy man named Jack Burke in 1972. Jack had served in the Army Air Corps before the military converted it to the Air Force. After serving in the Army Air Corps and the Air Force for several years, he switched over to the Navy and retired in 1970 as a journalist. Betty's son-in-law, Bobby Doyle, served in the Navy.

As a recruiting officer in the Naval Reserves, I enlisted my daughter, Lynn, into the Naval reserves in 1983; and she served for several years. Part of that was overseas in Rota, Spain. Her commitment to other things caused her to leave the reserves in 1985. I also enlisted my son, Larry, into the Navy in 1985; and he served in the Seabees for three years until an injury disqualified him for service. He was discharged in 1988.

David Eldridge, Pat's second son, enlisted in the Army reserves. He earned his master's degree in history and was commissioned as a second lieutenant. He has traveled to many parts of the world in his field of expertise; his specialty at that time was intelligence. At the time of this writing, January 2017, he remains in the active Army reserves and currently holds the rank of lieutenant colonel. He served in Iraq and/or Afghanistan.

Scott Eldridge, Pat's youngest son, served in the Army. He served in the first Iraq invasion in 1992 in the 101st Airborne Division. He returned home and was discharged. He then pursued a profession in the nursing field where he excelled in many ways.

Donnie Eldridge, Pat's grandson, joined the Air Force in 2005 and is still serving as of this writing. As one can see, our family has served the military very well and can be pleased that we have done our part of protecting our country in one way or another no matter what our specialty was.

Protecting our nation in the military is only one way to protect our freedom from hoods, gangsters, dope dealers, and others of their profession. We also owe a great debt of gratitude to our first responders, firemen, police officers, and last but not least, our highway patrol.

Gene's son, Kevin, started out as a rookie guarding a local college in Denver, Colorado. Over the years he has proven to be a liable asset to the state and has worked his way up to lieutenant colonel in the Colorado State Patrol. At the present, he is second in command and a great leader in accident reconstruction and the immigrations department. He hopes to retire in the near future, and we all wish him God's speed and happy retirement.

Michael, Kevin's son, is also a Colorado State Patrol and has the same area to patrol that Kevin had when he was a sergeant. Michael did very well in the academy, and God willing, he has a great future with the highway patrol. Bryan, Kevin's other son, is deputy sheriff in Mesa County, Colorado, and has also done well for himself. He also graduated from the academy with honors and, most recently, was chosen as a member of the Mesa County SWAT Team, which is a great honor within itself.

We are very proud of all the members of our family for serving their country in one way or another and making it safe and keeping it safe for our children, grandchildren, and our great-grandchildren. May God protect our boys in uniform regardless of which organization they belong to.

Although our dad did not serve in the military, he raised his family to have a deep conviction for our Lord and taught us the correct way to accomplish a task and to do it the correct way the first time. He taught us to work together and in unison so all tasks would be easier. Each of our family realizes that hard work never killed anyone and that one must *persevere* to accomplish his/her goal in life. It will not be handed to you on a silver platter; and as the "ole timers" would say, "There ain't no free lunches."

The following is a tribute to a wonderful family that we learned to love and appreciate early in life. We spent many days both on weekends and summer days with this family and loved every day of it. Uncle Artie and Aunt Evie were two of the most generous and kind people that I have ever known or have ever been associated with. My vocabulary is inadequate to describe my heartfelt thanks and appreciation to these two multi talented people. Aunt Evie was my grandfather's, Homer Eldridge, younger sister. We also spent a lot of time with my grandfather's other sisters family, Uncle Clarence and Aunt Sallie Mims. They were very gracious to us as well and treated us as on of their own They had six children: Lavada, Ollie, Dorothy, Lois, Shirley and Donald.

"Big Daddy" and
"Big Momma"

Growing up with all of these children I have determined that the parents have passed down their talents to each of their children in some way and fashion. It was with a sad heart that I have attended the funerals of most of my beloved cousins who I believe departed too soon for us but not for the Lord.

OUR TRIPS TO UNCLE
ARTIE'S AND AUNT EVIE'S

When we lived in Orlando, Florida after my parents divorced, we would come to Georgia to visit our relatives from time to time. One of our favorite homes was that of Uncle Artie and Aunt Evie Tompkins who lived on a farm owned by Mr. J.E. Ladson. They had ten children and lived in this large old farm house. There were six boys and four girls and they had three large bedrooms with two double beds in each and everyone had a special place to sleep. Four of the boys slept in one room, Uncle Artie and Aunt Evie slept in the adjoining room with each sleeping with one of the smaller children. The larger girls slept in a room across the hall; Next to their room was the dining room which had a long table with a chair at each end and two long benches for the children to sit on.

When daddy got off work at the base we would be ready to leave for Georgia as soon as he arrived home. This was in the middle forties and there were no interstate highways or short cuts from Orlando to Moultrie, it was all two lane roads and many small towns to travel through on this long journey. Daddy was the only driver so he did the best he could staying awake and doing a good job driving his 1936 Chevrolet four door sedan. There were four of us children, Aunt Betty Ann, me (Papa), Uncle Gene and Uncle Pat and daddy in this car. Aunt Betty would sit in the front and we three boys would have the back seat all to ourselves. One time daddy hit a bump in the road and Pat thought Gene had hit him so he hit Gene back. Never knew the difference.

We would arrive at their home about 2 AM in the morning and daddy would wake Uncle Artie up to let us in for the remaining of the morning. I would be put in the bed with two of the boys, Gene would be put in another bed with two other boys, Betty would be put in the bed with two of the girls and then Daddy would have a bed for him and Pat. This would be our sleeping arrangements for the weekend as well.

In the morning Aunt Evie and the older girls would arise and cook breakfast for all of us. Sometimes Uncle Artie would go fishing in the little creek behind his home and catch a lot of small brim which would be cleaned and fried whole for breakfast. Their dining table was very long so everyone would have a place to eat. Aunt Evie would always have grits, eggs and either ham or bacon, and then the fish. Homemade butter, milk and syrup were always a constant at their table as they had plenty of chickens and cows on the farm and Uncle Artie made the syrup himself.

This being Saturday morning Uncle Artie would get ready to go to town as he was the only one that went to town. He would take an opossum or two to town and sell them in certain areas as he had regular customers waiting for them. Reade, the eldest son would hitch the mules to a two mule wagon and load the corn that we had shucked and shelled to the grist mill in Berlin, Georgia for processing into grits, meal for cornbread. It would take us most of the morning to go to Berlin and back home. We would have to drive on the edge of the road because we didn't want to get hit by a car. The girls would have the chore of cleaning the yard of all debris, grass or anything else that may be there. The girls would also clean the house and do the scrubbing if necessary. They would us a handmade scrub brush to clean the floor. This scrub brush was made of old corn shucks bolted together between two small boards with a long handle. Their cleaning solution was lye soap and water which always did an excellent job.

During the summer school vacation Aunt Betty and I would come to stay with them and help work on the farm. We would work with the other children in tobacco, cotton and peanuts. We also had many other chores to perform because a farm cannot survive on its own. They many animals to attend to and make sure that they had plenty of food and water in their trough. Mules that they tended the land with and cows that provided milk and butter, pigs that they butchered for lots of their meat for breakfast and other mea'ls and chickens that provided eggs and on occasions Sunday dinner. We would shuck our corn and then process it through a Sheller to prepare it for the grist mill that we went to on Saturday.

During this time line Uncle Artie did not have appliances that we have today to make life better for the house wife and family. No refrigerators, washing machines, freezers or any of the kitchen appliances that we have today. The ladies cooked on wood burning stoves and prepared all the meals through manual operations and no electric appliances. Wood cutting normally was the job for the men folks since it was a bad chore to cut and split the wood so it would fit into the wood burning stove compartment. Some of the stove had a water compartment on the side where water was heated for kitche use, absolutely no electric water heaters at all. To preserve the meats from the animals that they killed and butchered for food, Uncle Artie had a small building behind the house near the kitchen that they call a "smoke house". In this small building he would hang the meat from rafter and build a fire in it so he could smoke or preserve the meat for long term keeping for the family's consumption later on.

Since there was no running water they had a well that was positioned next to the back porch and the water had to·be pulled up by buckets for all uses. There was a special bucket positioned on the back porch that we drank from by using a small aluminum dipper. Everyone used the same dipper and they also had another bucket of water in the kitchen that they mostly used for cooking and used some to wash dishes. Family members bathed in a large metal tub that was positioned on the back porch and normally the babies were washed first and then it was mostly a lottery as to who would bathe next. It was in this same tub that Uncle Artie would bathe each Saturday morning before he went to town. It was a known fact that nobody came to the back while he was bathing and getting ready for his trip to town.

Since there was no running water in the home, it was necessary that they have an outside toilet for everyone to go to when they needed to use the bathroom. This little house was not too far from the back porch but far enough that it was not a problem for anyone in the house. This is where I was introduced to a unisex bath room as all ages and sexes used the same place. This small building was large enough that two people could use the bathroom at the same time which was convenient and we called it a "two holer". For privacy, it at least had a lock on the inside to keep others from opening the door while it was in use.

There were not many toys around their home but they made things to play with to pass the time of day. The boys would take a tobacco can and nail it to a tobacco stick and push a round steel ring all over the yard for their recreation. Some would make sling shots and goes bird hunting to prove their skill at shooting. We would go fishing at the small creek down behind the house and just make our own recreation most of the time. We would play marbles sometime as most of us knew how to shoot pretty well and it was always fun to compete with our cousins. Lots of the times Gene would outshoot us and end up with most of the marbles but sometimes he would give them back later, I guess so he could win them back later on. There was a larger creek about a mile from their house that we called "Chapman's Wash Hole" and we would go there lots of afternoons to bathe and have a good recreational time with one another. We had no bathing suits so they called it "skinny dipping" in those days. No girls were allowed at this function.

We always had a great time visiting this family no matter if it was for a weekend or for the summer. From an outsider, you would have thought that we were a great big family because we always worked and played together very well. Uncle Artie and Aunt Evie never showed any partiality toward any of us.and made us feel like we wer.e all family. In years to come Uncle Artie was one of our greatest allies in solving family problems as they arose. One thing I do remember is that with all those children, plus Aunt Betty and me, I can never remember any of us having any large disagreements or fights as you in families today; and, never even saw the hint of a disagreement between Uncle Artie and Aunt Evie in all the years we stayed with them or during the latter years as we lived as neighbors. They were great neighbors and one of the most obliging families I ever saw or was around, always willing to help their neighbor.

Uncle Artie was a man of many talents, among those was one that he received a lot of notoriety about. It was hi.s ability to catch rattle snakes in the winter time. At one point in time Uncle Artie had over a hundred rattle snakes in captivity. He had this guy from The Ross Allen Farm in Florida that would come by periodicity to purchase them from him if the snakes were large enough; Ross Allen only wanted the large ones as he had a snake farm in Florida that he displayed them in for public viewing.

Uncle Artie and some of his sons would scout the area around the farm for gopher holes to determine if a snake had crawled in since their last visit. They would rake around the entrance of the hole and revisit it in a few days to look for tell-tell signs of snake movement. If there were signs of snake movement, they would take a rubber hose and stick down the hole and pour gasoline into it to run the snakes out. Once the snake came out, someone would grab the sriake with a long pole with a hook on the end to capture it in a safe manner. They would put the snake in a container to transport them to their storage building for safe keeping. There is no way of knowing how many snakes Uncle Artie and his sons caught over the years but it was a large number. The people in our area called Uncle Artie "The Rattle Snake Man" and that name stayed with him for a long time.

The Tompkins family was a great part in organizing our Eldridge reunion and keeping it going for so many years. I remember one year Uncle Artie was the oldest person at the reunion and he was 67 years old. His brother-in-law, Uncle William (Bill} Eldridge, Aunt Evie's brother, was one of the ones at the first reunion in 1967 which was held at the EMC building.

ABOUT THE AUTHOR

Homer J. Eldridge wrote this book after he was presented with a book entitled *Grandpa, Do You Remember When?* by his four great-grandsons: Christopher Eldridge, Bradley Warren, Cameron Eldridge, and Blake Warren. This was a comprehensive book requiring a lot of detail about the grandparent answering each question in the book. The book asked many questions that Homer could not limit the answers to the space provided in the book. He realized that it would take more space, so he designed his answers in the manner that is in his book. All questions are highlighted in bold print, and the answers are in a smaller print. Homer wanted to be as specific as possible so these four young men could understand his writing and the thought behind each answer. This was to be a part of their ancestry and needed to be as specific as possible. Homer added some short stories about various people related to these boys, and a couple were written by each of their mothers, Diana Eldridge Warren and Lisa Eldridge, that were inspirational articles at the time written. None of the tales or short stories is fictional but actually happened to their relatives.

Hopefully, this book will act as a connection from these young men to the past of Homer from his childhood to his older years in life. Homer was eighty-three years old when he completed the book. It took him about three years to write everything and to get it all organized as he wanted. The book was printed by a local printing office; and Homer has received many great reviews from his family, friends, and especially from his wife's doctors. Homer would write portions of the book and his wife, Virginia (Mema), would edit it for correctness. Homer's wife saw the final copy of the book but passed away shortly thereafter.